S-
M

Line Down!

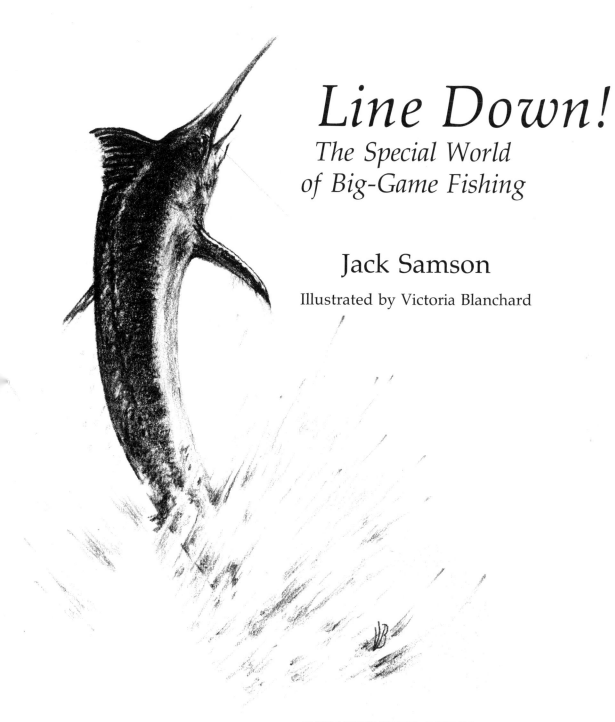

Line Down!
The Special World
of Big-Game Fishing

Jack Samson

Illustrated by Victoria Blanchard

WINCHESTER PRESS

Two of the chapters in this book, "The Blue Marlin" and "The Dolphin," appeared originally in slightly different form in **Field & Stream** *magazine. Grateful acknowledgment is made for permission to reprint them here.*

Copyright © 1973 by Jack Samson
All rights reserved

Library of Congress Catalog Card Number: 73-78814
ISBN: 0-87691-111-4

Published by Winchester Press
460 Park Avenue, New York 10022

Printed in the United States of America

This book is dedicated to those anglers—
both past and present—
who have not only loved the sea and the great fish,
but have written about them.

Foreword

*T*here's an old publishing homily that good editors do not make good writers, nor do skilled shooters
often display any outstanding talents in angling—and
vice versa. There are exceptions to both statements, but
rare indeed is the individual who wears four hats as a
first-class editor, an outstanding writer, an angler of
tournament caliber and a hunter of commensurate skill.
This is the briefest sketch of Jack Samson. Much of the
man as I know him you will discover on these salt-
soaked pages.

Fittingly, I first met Jack at that Temple of Tunadom,
the Cat Cay Club in the Bahamas. We fished together,
and since he is the kind of guy that people just automatically admire, I intended to see him more often; I did not

know that he would eventually join *Field & Stream* and that "seeing" him would become a professional habit. In the years since, we have shared everything from pan-fried bass on Pennsylvania's Susquehanna River to salmon on Scotland's Spey, and knowing the man is to recognize his angling philosophy—"There are no gray areas, just black and white."

Far from being a pretentious volume, *Line Down!* recreates a gut smell of twin diesels in a following sea, the squawk of gulls as they rise like confetti on the wind, the rainbow plume of a roostertail from a hull planing at full throttle, and those back-wrenching, arm-knotting hours when things go wrong on a giant tuna and you swear you'll never do *this* again. But you do, and you will, for as long as the fish run north and your working parts can still be scraped off barnacles.

A. J. McClane

Contents

Foreword by A. J. McClane   vii
Introduction   xi

one	*The Broadbill Swordfish*	1
two	*The Black Marlin*	11
three	*The Sailfish*	23
four	*The Blue Marlin*	29
five	*The Bluefin Tuna*	37
six	*The Dolphin*	53
seven	*The Special World*	65
eight	*A Green Fish*	75
nine	*The Striped Marlin*	85
ten	*The Barracuda*	95
eleven	*A Boat Is for Fishing*	105
twelve	*The Mako*	115
thirteen	*The Tarpon*	131

Appendix A: Equipment and Technique   145
Appendix B: The IGFA Rules   167

Introduction

Line Down! is not meant to be a big-game fishing textbook, although I have included some basic information in the Appendixes. It is a personal book based on my own experiences, and its intent is to let the reader — who may or may not have had similar experiences — share some of the best of mine.

The angler who does want to read more about the sport will find that there are many excellent books. There may never be a better book written on big-game fishing than *Salt Water Fishing* by the late great Van Campen Heilner, former associate editor of *Field & Stream*. Published in the 1930s, it still stands as a landmark in ocean-fishing literature. Also a classic is Harlan Major's *Salt Water Fishing Tackle*, long out of print. In recent times *Big*

Fish and Blue Water, by Australian angler and writer Peter Goadby, is the definitive book on fishing the Pacific.

There are other books on saltwater big-game fishing for those who want to learn the fine points of the sport — angling methods, boats, gear and tackle. It would be difficult to beat such prestigious texts as *Modern Salt Water Sport Fishing* by Frank Woolner, *Successful Ocean Game Fishing* edited by Frank Moss, and *Fishing with Lee Wulff;* such practical guides as *Sportfishing for Sharks*, by Frank Mundus and Bill Wisner; and the most monumental work of all on both freshwater and saltwater fish and fishing: *McClane's Standard Fishing Encyclopedia* by *Field & Stream's* longtime fishing editor, A. J. McClane.

There are also many books whose authors have filled me with pleasure, and envy perhaps, by writing so well about *their* experiences: Herman Melville in his wondrous *Moby Dick;* Zane Grey in *Tales of Fishes* and *Tales of Swordfish and Tuna;* Ernest Hemingway in a dozen stories; Kip Farrington in *Fishing the Atlantic* and *Fishing the Pacific;* Tommy Gifford in *Anglers and Muscleheads;* Henry (Hal) Lyman in many stories in his *Salt Water Sportsman* magazine; George Reiger in *Zane Grey, Outdoorsman;* and many others.

Fighting the big fish is one thing. Putting the experience on paper is another. It is the latter I have tried to do with this book, and I hope in some measure I have succeeded. *J. S.*

Line Down!

chapter one

The Broadbill Swordfish

My favorite memories of my father are of him on the sea. He should have been a ship's captain in the sailing days, because no man ever loved the sea more — whether he was pitching about on it in one of his many small boats or standing on a jetty and watching the waves smash against the rocks.

But he was not a captain. He was a newspaperman — like me. After graduating from Brown University — following a stint in France with the 103d Field Artillery of the Yankee Division in World War I — he took a job on the Providence *Journal* as an editorial writer. There were some other good writers on the old *Journal* in those days, and some good editors. A. J. Liebling was a reporter there with my father, and left following the crash to work for Barrett on the old New York *World*. But that's not getting us to the subject of the sea.

My father had a number of boats—a 16-foot mahogany Chris Craft I especially remember because it scared the devil out of my mother, brother and me when he would tear under the old Oakland Beach Bridge. That bridge has been gone since the hurricane of 1938, which altered the face of Buttonwoods so much. Buttonwoods was a summer colony where we lived each year.

But the boat I think my father liked the best was an Elco cruiser, which I believe was about 38 feet. She was an old secondhand craft and smelled good all over to me—the scent of calking, tar, gasoline, old paint and oily rags sort of exuded from her all the time. The single engine was cranky, and my father spent half his weekends down in the small engine room either swearing at the engine or banging it with a hammer or wrench.

One of his sailing pals was a man named White—I cannot remember his first name, but he was a fat man and liked beer in a big glass stein. Another man who used to go out with them was "Kickey" Hull, a longtime editor of the *Journal*.

The Elco had a harpoon walk on the bow, held rigid by steel cables, and the favorite pastime of my father and friends on summer weekends was to cruise the waters near Block Island for broadbill swordfish. In those days they were harpooned all the time, and I don't remember many people fishing for them with rod and reel. This was just before the Depression.

However, the old Elco had a cockpit astern and there was a folding metal fighting chair with rubber tips on the legs to keep it from sliding. There were two big rods my father kept in the forward cabin. I never knew what kind of reels were on them until after he died in the early 1960s. I found an old reel in an attic with some other things he had kept for a lifetime—like a German helmet from World War I with a silver spike on top. The reel was a 14/0 and the serial number was 732. It weighs almost 13 pounds with line on it, and the name on the handle reads "Edward Vomhofe, Maker, N.Y. Pat. May 20.02." The plate on the oil port next to the big handle reads "Edward Vomhofe, Maker, N.Y. Pat. July 14.96." It is made of German silver, and I still have it. I know who the Vomhofe brothers were, and I don't intend to sell the reel as long as I live.

My father did not take me or my brother out fishing with him very often because we were too young. I must have been about eight or nine then and my brother was two years younger. Besides, the old Army buddies always had cold beer and food along and they didn't want kids getting in the way of a good day's outing. But he did take me a couple of times, because I loved to fish for skipjacks, tautog and flounder. I never caught any big fish. Kids today use rods and reels a lot more than we did in those days. We would sail a little Beetle catboat across to East Greenwich and maybe drift in the middle of the bay using handlines and clams for bait. We used to catch a lot of weakfish—which were called squiteague in those days—close to an old wrecked ship off Oakland Beach. But a lot of our time was taken up with spearing eels and blueshell crabs to sell.

So it was a real thrill when my father announced one early Saturday morning—on a fine calm day in July—that he was going to take me with him and Mr. White to try for swordfish out of the bay near Block Island. He bought some cans of chum, which smelled pretty bad and must have been groundup moss bunker. Those he stored in the stern, and then he bought a couple dozen small mackerel, which he tossed in the ice chest. He used to fish some for sand sharks and always talked about catching a mako, but I don't remember him ever catching one—although he did catch some pretty big ones of other species, with a chum slick and mackerel for bait. I lay on the bow walk for a couple of hours as the old boat made pretty good time out of Narragansett Bay and finally passed Point Judith. The sun was warm on my back and I watched the bow waves curl back from the prow. A few miles from Point Judith—with my father and Mr.

White on the bridge—a school of porpoise suddenly showed up and played along just ahead and beside us. I can still see them on the glassy surface of the sea.

The ground swells began to pick up a bit shortly before noon and we all began a watch for basking swordfish. My father constantly swept the horizon with his battered binoculars. Occasionally another boat would pass us by, doing the same thing.

An hour or so later—with no sight of dorsal fins or tails on the surface—my father shut off the engine and went forward to get some sandwiches. I remember eating a cheese and ham sandwich with mustard on it and drinking a bottle of root beer. After sandwiches and beer, my father and Mr. White punched some holes in a can of rotten chum and lowered it over the stern on a line. The chum fanned out like an oil slick on the surface of the ocean for 100 feet back. The two men each hooked on a mackerel and let the baits drift astern in the slick. I climbed on top of the cabin to watch.

Half an hour or so later Mr. White got a strike and we had a great time as he finally cranked in a sand shark about five feet long. The mean-looking shark swam around and around next to the boat and my father tried to gaff it, but they finally decided it wasn't worth it and snipped the wire leader with a pair of cutters and put on another hook.

That was the last shark caught, and the swells were coming up a little and the wind was picking up slightly from seaward. Finally my father and Mr. White decided to look for some more swordfish to harpoon. I was glad of that, because just sitting and rising and falling on those swells wasn't making me feel any better. I felt a lot better when we got under way again, and I lay down on the bow to watch the prow cut the waves.

I was half asleep when I heard Mr. White yell, "Fin! Off the port bow!"

It sure was. There was a curved dorsal fin and a sickle-shaped tail fin about 200 yards away. My father came pounding up to the walk with a harpoon, which was fastened by a length of rope to a small wooden keg perched on the bow. Mr. White turned the boat and aimed straight for the fins. I could feel my heart pounding in my chest and in the sides of my head as we came closer and closer.

"Son," my father said sharply, "get back from the bow and stay away from those coils of line."

I know now why he said so, but I wasn't too sure then. If a man gets tangled in a harpoon line he will be pulled down and drowned.

We were about 15 feet from the fish—which never seemed to notice us at all—when my father heaved the harpoon at it.

The harpoon went right over the fish's back and the line touched the dorsal fin. That fish exploded the surface and splashed water all over us as it went down.

"I'll be goddammed!" said my father.

"Jesus, Harry!" said Mr. White. "That was one hell of a fish!"

"I'll be goddammed!" my father said again, slowly pulling in the harpoon rope and coiling it up again on the bow.

We cruised around again and didn't see another fish for quite a while. We had about decided to start back at about 3:00 p.m. when my father saw a fin again off to the port side. It looked a lot smaller than the other one—even to me.

"Harry," said Mr. White to my father, "what do you say we try to catch the son of a bitch on the rod and reel?"

"What for?" asked my father.

"Well, hell," said Mr. White. "The way you throw that harpoon we're never going to do any good. Besides"—he took a large swallow of beer from his glass stein—"I never saw one caught on rod and reel. McCord over at Barrington caught one last week and I'll never hear the end of it."

My father looked at the fish on the surface.

"I don't know," he said slowly. "How did he do it?"

"According to him, he trolled a mackerel past its nose and the damn thing just grabbed it."

"The hell you say," said my father.

5

"Eyah," said Mr. White.

"Well," said my father, reaching in the ice chest and taking out a mackerel about a foot long, "no harm in trying. How did he rig it?"

"He said through the lips, so's its mouth stayed shut," said Mr. White.

"Umm," said my father, passing the hook through the mouth of the mackerel. "OK, take her past that damn fish, but don't go too close. I'm going to let out a lot of line so we don't scare it. If it doesn't work then we can still try the harpoon."

Mr. White nodded and we began a large circle, my father letting out line with the big reel as we moved. The mackerel made a skipping motion on the surface and a V-shaped wake spread out from it. I wasn't nearly as excited as I had been when the first fish showed up.

"Slow her down a little," said my father as the bait neared the basking swordfish. "I think it's moving a little fast."

"OK," said Mr. White, easing back on the throttle a bit. "Jesus, Harry," he said tensely, "the damn thing is going to pass right in front of its snout!"

"I don't have much faith in this business," my father said as he looked at Mr. White. "I think the harpoon is a lot better."

I was watching the fish on the surface and I can still see the way that tail lashed once. The fish didn't move more than ten feet before it hit that trolled mackerel. The next sound I heard was the shriek of the big reel in my father's hands. The fish was moving off slowly—still on the surface.

"Holy Christ!" I heard my father shout. "The damn thing took it!"

He yanked upright on the big rod and the fish disappeared in a shower of spray—only to appear a moment later heading straight up into the air.

I almost fell off the side of the gunwale.

"My God!" Mr. White yelled, jamming the engine into forward. "Hang onto him, Harry!"

My father didn't say anything. His face was set in a

funny look and his lips were straight. He had the butt of the big rod stuck into his stomach.

"Ease off, ease off!" he screamed at Mr. White, adjusting the big star drag on the reel at the same time. "This fish is tearing my arms out of the sockets!"

Mr. White slipped the control into neutral and then reverse as the swordfish came out of the water again in an arching leap that froze me to the side of the cabin.

The big reel was singing a song of protest and the fish was making leap after leap. I can see it all again as though it were yesterday. My father never thought of the metal fighting chair. He just hung onto that big rod, and the fish kept jumping and jumping until I thought it would never stop. Mr. White kept yelling advice about keeping the rod tip up, easing off on the drag and watching the direction of the line. I couldn't do anything but watch.

It seemed like hours before the fish stopped jumping and finally began swimming in gradually decreasing circles around the boat. My father walked him around the boat for what seemed like another hour until it was close to the boat on its side.

"Now what the hell are we going to do with it?" he asked Mr. White.

"Jesus, Harry," Mr. White said. "I don't know. Maybe the big gaff will hold. You want me to try?"

"Somebody better try," my father said. "I'm about done. This rod butt has taken half the skin off my stomach. For Chrissakes somebody dip a bucket of water out and throw it over me before I pass out!"

"Jackie," Mr. White said, "do what your dad said."

I grabbed a bucket and doused my father completely—clothes and all. "Aahhhh," was all he said.

Mr. White left the control in neutral and picked up the big long-handled gaff. "OK, Harry," he said slowly. "I'm going to try. As soon as I sink this hook into him, drop that rod and try and get a line on him."

My father nodded and heaved as hard as he could. The big fish came alongside—gasping and lying flat in the water. Mr. White reached out and sank the big gaff into its belly. It must have paralyzed the fish for a moment, because it didn't do anything but sort of hump up. Meanwhile my father grabbed a line, leaned over the gunwale, slipped the line around the thin part of the fish near the tail and snubbed it around a big stern cleat. About then the fish came out of shock and started thrashing. I ran around trying to help, but nobody noticed me.

There was a lot of water coming into the boat and there was a lot of shouting—some words I never heard before—and much grunting and hanging on. It seemed a long time before that fish quit fighting. Finally both Mr. White and my father managed to slide the swordfish over the side and it landed with a big thumping noise in the boat. I never saw such a fish!

After a few whacks with a heavy wooden club it quit thrashing and lay still. My father picked me up and swung me around. Then he and Mr. White did a funny dance in the cockpit. Then they drank a lot of beers from the big glass steins. The sea was coming up pretty high and I was not feeling too good, but they kept pounding each other on the back and laughing. I finally crawled up into the forward cabin and lay down.

The old boat took a long time to get back—what with a following sea and it finally getting dark. I remember hearing a lot of singing, songs with words like "Pack up your troubles in your old kit bag and smile, smile, smile," "It's a long way to Tipp . . ." something . . . It was all pretty hazy. We stopped in North Kingston for piss clams—which I didn't want—and then some johnnycakes—very late at night.

My mother was real mad when we got home. I don't remember what time it was. But I remember the big fish hung up on a dock back in the cove behind Buttonwoods and a lot of people coming down to see it—even in the dark.

It's a funny thing. That's the only swordfish I have ever seen caught. I've fished for them off Montauk until my eyes ached. I've trolled around the damned things until I could have shot at them with a rifle—and they

never would take the bait. I've trolled deep for them off
Ft. Lauderdale at night where skippers have sworn they
could catch me one—and never a bite. I've trolled for
them off Catalina Island, where Zane Grey caught them
by the dozens—and I never got one to strike.

And I am beginning to think I never will catch one.
But it doesn't really matter—because I saw one caught
and that will last me a lifetime.

chapter two

The Black Marlin

I had caught a couple of sailfish off Miami while stationed at 36th St. Airport during World War II. There were a number of us in my anti-submarine squadron who liked to fish, and the six-week celestial-navigation course the Army Air Corps insisted all air crews take did not use up all our time. Some of us managed to get out to the Tamiami Canal for bass on a flyrod and on other days chartered sportfishing boats to go out into the Gulf Stream. I don't remember being particularly impressed with catching sails then—perhaps because the excitement of being in the big war overshadowed everything else.

But I do remember the first marlin I caught, and it was a long way from Florida. A good many years later—

after a stint as a wire-service reporter for United Press in the Korean War—I was en route to the States for a welcome leave. I had gotten a bellyful of the big Pan Am stratocruiser which seemed to drone on forever from Tokyo to Wake Island and then to Honolulu. It was during a forced stopover for repairs in Hawaii that I decided to tour the islands just savoring the hot sun and lush vegetation on the big island. I came to the town of Kailua-Kona and walked out to look at a fleet of charter boats. My plane wasn't going to leave until the next day.

It was about ten in the morning and most of the boats were out, but there was one old wooden Owens lashed to the pilings. The skipper had just come up from the open hatch with an oily rag and was wiping his hands. His Hawaiian mate was asleep in the shade of the battered canvas top. The skipper looked like a refugee from the *African Queen*—a real Bogart type.

"I don't suppose," he said, eyeing me as if I were a Coast Guard inspector, "that you might want to go out fishin'."

I looked at the old boat. It looked to be about 32 feet.

"How come you couldn't get a charter this morning?" I said.

"Engine got cranky. I needed a new head gasket. Took me a couple of hours to fix it."

I noticed the outriggers were in good shape, the battered fighting chair was rigged with a sturdy harness and the boat generally looked as though it had been well cared for. A couple of stout rods held old but shiny Ocean City reels.

"What you charge for the day?" I asked.

The skipper looked at the bay for a moment. "Normally eighty bucks," he said, "but since you won't get a whole day, fifty."

I grunted and leaned against a post.

"What's the sea like?"

"This side of the island is always in the lee. It's only a few miles out."

"What we after?"

I noticed the mate had opened his eyes and was slowly getting up.

"Marlin," said the skipper. "Stripes, blacks and blues. Might pick up some sails, maybe a wahoo. Plenty of big dolphin. Never can tell."

"When can you leave?" I asked.

By this time the mate was busily polishing the brass on the old compass.

"How's two minutes strike you?" said the skipper. "She's fueled up."

"Where's all your bait?"

"Aboard. You might pick up some beer if you've a thirst. There's ice aboard and enough canned stuff to make a lunch."

I glanced at the rental car parked near the end of the dock. "The car all right?"

"Nobody will bother it," said the skipper. "Hop aboard. Kioshi here will get a case of beer while we get the lines off. I got some old clothes in case you don't want to get those fancy slacks all covered with billfish blood." That did it.

By the time the Hawaiian-Japanese mate got back with a case of American canned beer, the skipper had the engine turning over and all lines cast but a stern and bow line looped over a piling. I had slipped on a pair of faded suntan pants and an old T-shirt from a forward locker. My feet slid a bit inside a pair of ragged old boat sneakers, but I couldn't have cared less. It took us very little time to get out of the harbor and into blue water. The mate was all over the boat—getting the outriggers out, rigging wire leaders and putting beer on ice. By the time we hit the fishing area he had made me a corned beef and mustard sandwich and handed me a cold beer. The seas were only about two feet in the lee of the big island and the rugged coast to the east loomed mistily in the noon sunlight. I could see several boats north of us, all trolling.

The mate placed both big rods in the gunwale holders and checked the strike drags. The lines looked heavy, and I suspect now—since that long-past day—that they were braided linen. One was slightly smaller than the other and I would guess that they were 24-thread and 39-thread lines—about equal to our modern 80-pound and

130-pound lines. The reason I say that is that the wire leaders were both 30 feet long and the IGFA required leaders that long for the big lines. Also you never know in Hawaiian waters when you will encounter a big marlin. It was considered smart to use the heavy tackle on all big-game fish. After all, it was far better to catch a 30-pound wahoo on 130-pound line than to loose a 600-pound blue marlin on 15-thread line—about equal to our present-day 50-pound-test lines.

Kioshi came out of the cabin with a couple of strange-looking plugs, about 12 or 15 inches long, and laid them on top of the ice chest.

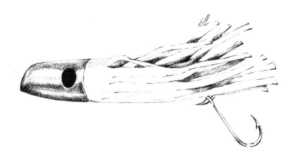

"Teaser plugs?" I asked, remembering the teasers used off Miami and Mazatlán for sailfish.

"No sir," he said, handing me one. "We use these to catch the billfish here. Dead bait don't work too good off these islands."

I looked at the one he had handed me. It was heavy and looked as though it had been made from a combination of wood and chrome. The face was flat and was made of the shiny metal, with a hole drilled through the entire length of both the metal and the wood. The body might have been made from a broomstick handle, and a length of cable leader ran through the entire thing. The cable looked like it might have a test strength of about 500 pounds. One end held a swivel to be fastened to the wire leader and the other held a hook of about 10/0 size. The tail end of the plug was festooned with a skirt made from lengths of red rubber. I later found out the skirt was made from an inner tube. The plug slid free on the leader and the single hook was not fastened to the plug. The other plug was a little smaller and was rigged with a single hook of about 8/0 size and carried a skirt of both red and green rubber. Both plugs were painted—mine blue with a red and black eye and the smaller one white with a black and blue eye set well back on the wooden body.

The mate fastened both plugs to the wire lines and ran them out and back of the boat on the port and starboard outriggers—where they dived and churned in the slight chop of the blue sea. Each time they dived beneath the surface they left a trail of bubbles 15 or 20 feet long before they surfaced and gulped enough air in the slanted and curved face and hollow core of the body to make more bubbles. I watched them for about five minutes as we droned along the coast, idly wondering when the skipper was going to throttle back to trolling speed. Finally I nudged the mate, who was honing down the point of a large flying gaff.

"When do we start trolling?" I shouted over the rumble of the engine.

"We trolling now," he shouted back. "Not like States. Eight to ten knots here is trolling speed."

I thought back to the Florida and Mexico fishing. The speed must have been no faster than four or five knots.

"Isn't that too fast for billfish?" I asked.

"Maybe in States," the mate grinned. "Not here. Billfish here hit these because mad. Not hungry."

I settled back in the fighting chair. What the hell, I thought. When in Rome. Besides, all I would be out was fifty bucks, and just getting out on the ocean for half a day was worth that. Besides, maybe we would luck into a wahoo, which I knew would hit fast lures.

I was dozing in the warm sunlight an hour or so later when the captain came down from his bridge and turned the wheel over to the mate.

"Mind if I have one of your beers?" he asked, reaching into the chest.

I nodded. "I couldn't drink a case if I wanted to," I said. "What's this business of trolling at eight knots for billfish? They don't hit balao baits or rigged mackerel at this speed in the States."

The skipper swallowed half a can of beer and wiped his mouth with the back of a salt-encrusted hand.

"They also don't catch blue marlin in the thousand-pound class and blacks close to two thousand." He smiled. "These monsters ain't interested in tidbits. When they want to eat they pick up a yellowfin of a hundred pounds or better. Ever try to troll a hundred-pound tuna?"

I shook my head.

"Well," he said, finishing off the can and reaching for another, "they mostly only take trolled baits that either make them mad or make them curious. That's why we pull these gadgets. They will take trolled live bait sometimes—bonito and the like—but is too much trouble catching the bait."

"What do you make them of?" I asked. "Or do you buy them?"

"Oh, I buy a couple from some other skippers who like to make them, but mostly I make my own. Kioshi here likes to make them too. The metal heads come from all sorts of stuff—like chrome bathroom towelracks and that sort of thing."

I watched the starboard plug jump and splash about 30 feet astern and the other doing the same thing about 60 feet back.

"Why the eyes painted on it?" I asked.

He laughed. "Hell, I don't know. Half the captains have some theory or other about it—like how far back they should be placed. But I'll tell you one thing: it's damn seldom a billfish hits one of these plugs when it doesn't have eyes!"

I grunted and opened another cold beer.

Another hour passed, and the mate came down and hauled in the plugs. He switched one and put on a black plug with a silver head and large white eyes set far back on the body. Then he tossed it back to ride as the far-out port bait.

I was rubbing some suntan lotion on the bridge of my nose a few minutes later when the mate let out a yell that froze me upright in the chair.

"Aiieee!" he shouted. "Here he comes!"

I barely had time to wipe the lotion off my palms on the slacks when the line snapped from the outrigger clip on the starboard side and the plug disappeared in an explosion of spray. I grabbed the rod and the mate shaded his eyes to look astern. I could already feel the fish taking out line, but being new at big-game fishing, I waited.

"Hit him! Dammit, hit him!" The captain screamed from the bridge. "He's hooked!" I leaned back and struck as hard as I could.

"Not that hard, goddammit!" the skipper shouted. "You want to break the rod?" I barely heard him because the water burst open astern and a multicolored, blunt-headed torpedo took off across the choppy surface in a dazzling series of jumps. "Mahimahi!" yelled Kioshi. "A big one! Aiieee, look at him go!"

It was a beautiful dolphin, I knew *that* much. But it was the first time I had ever heard it called mahimahi. It put up a fine fight but was no match for the big rod or heavy thread line. It took about ten minutes to subdue it, mostly because I wanted to savor the fun of fighting it. Kioshi finally gaffed it and we guessed its weight at about 40 pounds.

"Make a good meal," he said as he slid it into the fish box. I smiled and sat back down in the chair. As far as I was concerned, the day was already a success.

"Sorry about that strike," I said to the skipper, who grimaced but didn't smile.

"I guess I got a little excited."

"Well," he finally shouted down, "don't worry

about it. Everybody gets excited. I didn't know what it was. You couldn't have broken that rod on a dolphin, at least not on *that* fish, but it might have been a big marlin and those damn rods are expensive. Break one and there goes my profit for the day. Kioshi!'' He waved at the mate. ''Take the wheel a minute.''

He climbed down and took one of the rods from the holder. He jerked the line from the clip and held the rod parallel to the horizon and pointed straight back. He eased off the drag until the spool was turning slowly.

''When you get that strike,'' he said to me, ''point the tip at the spot and wait until you feel the fish's weight. When you do, hit him like this.'' He jerked the rod three times up at about a 45-degree angle. ''That should set any hook,'' he said. ''Don't lean into it and pull it back all the way as hard as you did. You don't have to. Got it?'' I nodded and he rigged the line back through the clip and slid the rod into the holder. That may have been one of the best pieces of fishing advice I ever got. I never forgot it.

The skipper took another beer and climbed back to the bridge. Kioshi grinned at me and leaned over to work on a harness buckle.

''Old man, he don't give free advice much.'' He winked at me. ''It don't hurt to listen to what he says. He damn good skipper. Catch a hell of a lot of marlin.'' I settled back in the chair. ''Hell,'' I said. ''I can take any advice you guys got. I don't know a thing about this game.''

''You do pretty good on mahimahi,'' Kioshi said seriously. ''You handle rod good. You never catch marlin before?''

''No,'' I said. ''Couple of sailfish, some small tuna, but never marlin.''

''Huh,'' he said. ''You got one damn good time comin'!''

''I sure hope so,'' I said and resumed the watch.

The marlin came up about thirty minutes later. It came up fast and I never saw it—since we were trolling slightly east and the late-afternoon sun glinted off the water where the plugs skipped. The first thing I knew was when the skipper let out a scream. "Right rigger!" he shouted. "Billfish!"

I couldn't see the fish and I couldn't remember where the right outrigger was—thinking my right was the left facing forward.

"Marleen!" yelled the mate, and I heard the line snap from the rigger clip.

"Line down!" yelled the captain at the top of his voice. "Goddammit, somebody grab that rod!"

The mate, thank God, grabbed the correct rod from the gunwale and shoved it into my hands. I jammed it into the seat gimbal, and as everything suddenly began to go into slow motion—as it always does with me and the big fish—I remembered to point the rod tip at the fish.

I felt the old boat surge forward as the skipper jammed his throttle full ahead to take up any slack. I was just beginning to feel a bit of weight when I heard the captain.

"Hit him, hit him, for Christ's sake hit him!"

To my everlasting credit I did exactly as I had been told and struck three times. That was the last move I made that made any sense to me. Right after that I saw the most beautiful fish I had ever seen come out of the sea behind me—and I can see it today silhouetted against that rugged coast of Hawaii, hanging in the air, twisting and writhing with rage at the bite of the hook.

"He's on! He's on!" screamed the skipper, slowing the boat down. "Don't let him get any slack. They don't swallow these plugs. Reel, reel!"

It never occurred to me to do anything except stare at that great leaping, thrashing fighting monster that was throwing spray over the ocean surface.

I didn't have to reel to take up slack, fortunately. That marlin made one towering leap after another, tearing line off the old Ocean City reel as though it were sewing thread. The reel had been set at strike drag, probably at about 30 pounds.

"Aiieee!" screamed Kioshi. "Marleen . . . look at heem go!"

That battle, which they told me later lasted about

forty-five minutes, was a complete blur to me. I still re-member parts of it—my right arm going dead cranking that big reel handle and continuing to crank long after all feeling had left it. I didn't know enough then to keep my left arm straight and let the kidney harness and my legs absorb the punishment. I kept trying to gain line by pulling on the rod with my left arm at the same time I was reeling—not knowing enough to crank as the rod is lowered rather than while it is being raised. It didn't matter. The mate kept swinging the chair to face the fish, which made several greyhounding runs and Lord knows how many more leaps before the skipper backed down on it in the choppy sea.

I dimly remember—through the pain of my arms and back—seeing the double line and big brass swivel come up several times and catching a glimpse of the wire leader. But each time the fighting fish would thrash across the surface and the mate would have to let go of the line.

Finally there was the blur of a gaff, the sound of the skipper landing on the deck to help and the shower of water over me as the marlin was gaffed again and held against the side of the hull. I didn't know enough to help tail-rope the fish and just sat in the chair, exhausted, as the two hauled the fish over the starboard gunwale. It landed with a slithering thump on the deck and the mate whacked it several times on the forehead with a wooden club.

And after that everything was a melee of slaps on the back, handshakes, whoops, grins, shouts and the headiest feeling I had ever felt, up to that day, in my en-tire life.

And there was suddenly a need to lean over the side—my stomach wrenching and the bitter taste of bile and beer in my mouth. When I stopped and slid back to the deck the skipper slapped me on the back and poured a cold can of beer over my head.

"Don't worry about it, son," he shouted. "Nothing to be ashamed of. You whipped hell out of that fish, but there ain't anybody who whips a black marlin in this world that's won an easy fight!"

And a black marlin it was. Not a Pacific blue as were most of the ones caught off Kailua-Kona, nor a striped marlin. It wasn't a big fish, now that I know how much black marlin weigh. It was 378 pounds, the dockmaster said later. I couldn't have cared less.

My arms, legs and back were sore for a week and I couldn't get out of bed for days without groaning. But that fish did something to me, and I really am not sure yet whether I am blessed or cursed because of it.

It made me an incurable big-game fisherman, that magnificent black marlin. May God rest its fighting soul.

chapter three
The Sailfish

Sometimes it is difficult to remember one's first catch of a particular species of big-game fish. But there was one sailfish I took in the late 1950s off the west coast of Mexico that will remain etched in my memory for many years.

The station wagon hummed along U.S. 85 south to Hatch, New Mexico, then to Deming, then across the border of Arizona late in the afternoon, south of Tucson that night and finally to the border of Mexico late in the evening. Art and Vince and I took turns driving. After passing through customs — a strictly routine matter which took only a few minutes — we headed south for Hermosillo. It was early in the morning when we passed through that Mexican town and, spelling each other, we kept on. As the sun rose July 6, we entered Guaymas, Mexico, perched on the sheer slopes of cholla cactus and rock-covered foothills at the edge of the Gulf of California. The water was as blue as the Mexico skies, and the surf looked like an oasis to three parched souls who felt as though they had been crawling across the Sahara for eight weeks on their hands and knees.

The first thing we did—after sixteen straight hours of driving—was to run down to the white curving beach and plunge into the almost lukewarm surf. I don't remember when anything ever felt as wonderful as that ocean after the 800 miles of New Mexico, Arizona and Mexico desert.

We didn't go out for sails that first day. In the first place we needed some sleep. So, later in the afternoon, we rented a 16-foot aluminum boat with a 40-horse outboard and went out to check the coastline and the general scenery. We took some light tackle and trolled off the jagged gull-and-pelican-covered islands offshore. We took several small grouper and a couple of bonito which fought well for their weight.

The next morning, we started out in all seriousness. Both Vince and I spoke Spanish, after a fashion. This did make things a little easier, but it certainly was not necessary. Almost all the boat owners and some boat captains spoke English. One was expected to do a little bargaining about the cost of a boat per day, depending on the number of avid fishermen about, the weather, the humor of the boat crew, the need of the boat owner, the preponderance of fish being caught and the budget of the fisherman. The price of a good diesel or gasoline cabin cruiser will vary. A higher price means a new, fiberglass boat and a few more knots, and the cheaper price usually means a rather older boat. Nevertheless, a seaworthy old job and *quien sabe?* Maybe it has a smarter captain and first mate when it comes to stalking sails.

We decided to alternate in the fighting chairs and split the cost. That way nobody would get bored with the dull periods and everybody had about an equal chance to nail the big ones. Tossing for the first chance at

24

the chairs and whether one wanted the right or left seat was our way of doing it. We did this every day for six days. That way nobody had any gripes when he missed his fish because of some arbitrary decision. We used a different boat and crew each day.

And miss fish we did. We had eight sails on and boated two the first day. The largest was a good one, 110 pounds. I still think that was an accident, but I'm not going to argue the point too much because I was the one who caught it.

Every boat captain and his mate had his own system of fishing for the sails. Each rigged the mullet bait a different way—some running the hook down through the head of the bait and others burying the hook deep in the fish and sewing it up with twine.

Some skippers seemed to like the baits closer in than others, and even the angle of the outriggers changed with boats. The teaser plug ran fairly deep—several yards below the surface. The first day out, a wild sail flashed up from nowhere, took the teaser plug and a length of stout line and went skipping across the surface of the ocean in a series of breathtaking leaps. Needless to say, both fishermen in the chairs thought they had the fish on and set hooks into thin air. We all saw sailfish before they struck the baits. They would come up behind the skipping mullet, the black dorsal fin would cut the surface first, and the fish would strike the bait. Naturally, this would trip the line from the outrigger and the line would fall slack into the sea. At this moment, the skipper would throttle the engine down to idle and we would wait. The sail would take the bait to a certain depth and then stop. The fisherman would put his thumb gently on the reel so he could tell when the big fish stopped. When it stopped, it was to turn the bait around in its mouth and begin to swallow it. If the big fish didn't feel the nip of the hook or the faint pull of the line, or become suspicious of some other aspect of the bait, the mullet would slide down its gullet, and the sail would begin to swim away. As to when to strike, it was all a matter of knowing sailfish. We depended entirely on the mates. They would stand over us and watch the reel—counting slowly to themselves in Spanish—then suddenly they would slap us on the shoulder and say "Now!"

The reason we missed most of the sails was simply that we couldn't wait until the skipper said "Now!" It just seemed inconceivable that the big fish could take that long to be hooked. The first sail I lost, I counted to seven and threw on the brake and struck. The big fish came out of the ocean 100 yards astern with the hook stuck in the hard cartilage of its mouth. In two jumps the hook came free and I sat staring at the slack line like an idiot. The skipper shook his head sadly.

Vince lost one sail when it came up, took the bait, went down, started to swallow it, then changed its mind and spit it out just as he struck. Art lost one which grabbed the bait, let it go and never did touch it again. He lost another which just wasn't hooked well and threw the hook after the third or fourth jump. I missed another which opened its mouth to take the bait, then changed its mind and disappeared—why, we will never know.

Vince set the season record for a pelican which grabbed his bait in spite of all the shouting and arm-waving we did to frighten it away.

A dolphin caught by Art weighed 26 pounds, leaped all over the ocean and put up one of the greatest fights I have ever seen. It came slashing in from an angle, took one of the baits and went straight up in the air, beginning a series of jumps that left us all speechless. As far as Art was concerned, after a twenty-minute battle a dolphin is a match for a sail anytime.

I got my biggest sail the fourth day out. It was the quietest angling day we had had all week. The sea was rough, and by late in the afternoon the man who was not in a fighting chair was napping between turns to fish. Art and I were in the chairs and it was about three-thirty. I was in the right-hand chair and, weary from watching the skipping baits, I was watching another fishing boat several miles away. I never saw the sail take the bait. Art did. Later he said all he saw was a huge shape come up from the depths behind the bait, and suddenly the bait was gone.

Art yelled "Sail!" and the line fell slack from the outrigger clip. At the yell, the skipper, Joe Morales, chopped the throttle back and jumped down behind me. The mate grabbed Art's rod and began hauling in his line. I sank the handle of the rod into the metal cup of the seat and braced myself.

I looked up at Joe. He shook his head slowly and put his thumb on the reel. It was turning slowly. Suddenly it stopped. Joe grunted to himself. The world seemed to have come to a stop. Each second seemed like hours. My mouth was dry and my hands wringing wet. Suddenly, the reel spool began to turn, ever so slowly. Then it began to let out line, still slowly, but gradually gaining speed.

Joe began counting to himself under his breath, "*Uno, dos, tres* . . ." I reached for the brake. ". . . *ocho, nueve* . . ." Never has time passed so slowly. Suddenly, when he reached the count of 13 he slapped me hard on the left shoulder and shouted. "*Ahora!* Hit him!" I flipped on the brake and struck.

The reel screamed, the rod went only about halfway back as the weight of the fish took up the slack and my arms straightened.

The surface of the ocean suddenly seemed to explode, and a great, unbelievable, silver, blue, purple and iridescent sailfish came hurtling straight up into the air. About 15 feet up it began a series of contortions—trying to throw the hook. Falling back with a tremendous splash, the huge fish shook its head wildly and leaped again. Later, the rest of them told me the sail leaped nine times before sounding. I don't know. All I clearly remember is those first two. They will remain with me forever.

After the fish went for the depths, the work began. Vince grabbed a bucket and rope, dropped it over the side, filled it with water and poured it over me every five minutes. He kept that up the whole hour and a half or so until the fish was boated. It probably saved my life.

When the fish finally tired, the mate reached down, took it by the bill and tapped it once on the forehead. It always seems unbelievable that a fish which fights that long and so spectacularly can die so easily. But it simply quivered once and died. Another always astonishing thing to me is the way the blues, golds, purples and silver colors fade to a solid black in a matter of seconds after the death of the fish. It weighed out at 138 pounds later.

Vince and his sailfish? It won't set any records, but then it didn't have to. It skittered across the surface of the sea just as though Zane Grey had ordered it for him, personally. It never quit fighting until its great heart stopped.

chapter four
The Blue Marlin

*I*t had been at least two hours since anything had come up to look at the baits. Earlier we had taken several dolphin along a weed line. Those most beautiful fish had put up a slashing, leaping, high-speed battle. Each fight's end was marked by the dolphin's incredible cobalt-blue, dark-green, yellow, and silver colors fading to black only moments after the fish was boated.

Pat had taken an acrobatic sail which made more than a dozen soaring leaps before coming alongside, where the mate cut the wire leader after tagging the fish. Following that, I hooked a streaking wahoo that put up a stubborn underwater fight but never broke the surface.

Billfish — either the white or the blue marlin — were our primary goal, but except for one small white that had

come up to examine and reject the three baits being trolled behind the sportfisherman, we had seen no more action. Half-dozing in the fighting chair, I watched the two outrigger baits and the one on the flat line directly astern skip and splash across the slight chop of the sea off Chub Cay in the Bahamas. The mate had put out a rigged mullet on the starboard outrigger. The outfit on that side had 30-pound-test line on the reel. The other outrigger held a mackerel—our bait for the big blue marlin. That reel held 50-pound-test monofilament. A balao bait was being used on the flat line, which held 20-pound-test mono.

We were trolling with the slight breeze off the port quarter, the two-foot chops giving us a slight roll and pitch as we moved on a southwesterly heading.

"Billfish!" came the skipper's shout from the Bimini tower, where he stood at the wheel about eight feet above the level of the cockpit deck.

"Which bait?"

"The mackerel on the port rigger," he shouted back. "He came up and took a look, but his dorsal fin or tail never broke the water. He went down, and I can't see him now, but watch out! He looked pretty interested."

Pat climbed into the tower with his camera. The mate suddenly pointed to the same bait on the port side.

"Here he comes!" he shouted.

The captain yelled, "Watch him!" and at that instant both the dorsal fin and bill of a marlin surfaced directly behind the mackerel. There was a vicious explosion of white water as the big fish slashed at the bait, knocking the line from the outrigger clip.

"Line down!" the skipper shouted, and I yanked the rod from its holder and lowered the tip almost horizontally, pointing at the spot where the fish had struck. The butt of the rod was jammed into the leather belt cup as the speed of the boat quickly took up the slack. The marlin should have been mouthing the bait, which he probably picked up after slashing or stunning it with his bill. The big fish's weight suddenly straightened the line, and it was on. I jerked the rod almost upright with three quick, short movements to set the hook just as the skipper shouted, "Hit him!"

The chair was hot from the sun. The metal butt fit easily into its chair gimbal. Then came the moment—as tense as any in sports—of waiting for the hooked billfish to break the surface.

Several hundred yards back, the surface of the ocean was shattered into a massive shower of white spray as a magnificent blue marlin, its rich blues, lavender stripes and silver flanks glistening in the bright sunlight, hurled itself into the air, twisting with rage at the bite of the hook.

The great, vibrant fish seemed to remain suspended for a brief moment before falling back to the surface in a geyser of white water, only to reappear in an instant with its second furious leap. The 50-pound-test tore off the screaming reel as if hooked to another boat going away from us at full speed. There were 700 to 800 yards of line on the reel and the marlin was only about 200 yards out, but it was difficult not to feel that the fish would take every foot of line on that first run. The power and unbelievable speed of these great fish make even the best of modern rods and reels feel like inadequate children's toys in the first few moments of battle. The skipper, Pat, and the mate were shouting at the spectacular fight of the fish. It was then that I found myself coaxing, challenging, and shouting encouragement to an adversary that had most of the advantages already on its side.

Falling back again with a slapping sound that we could hear in the cockpit, the blue came out once more and started tailwalking across the surface. It is difficult to appreciate the strength needed for a billfish to do this. The marlin stayed above the surface by using only the immense strength of its tail. The rest of the body did not appear to touch the surface at all, and the fish moved across the waves at an unbelievable speed.

The reel spool continued to screech, and there was that recurring uneasy feeling that approximately 800 yards was not going to be enough to stop this fish. Fifty-pound-test line can wear down good-sized marlin if used by someone familiar with billfish tactics, but 80-pound-test is far more practical for a novice to use. My favorite is 30-pound-test braided line, but I'm not bragging—liking it has cost me a number of blue marlin, simply because of my idiotic mistakes in handling the fish and tackle, mistakes that all big-game fishermen know about and make too often.

The marlin had stopped its tail-walking run after about 50 yards and then began a series of greyhounding leaps that are named for just what they look like—the leaping, stretched-out moves of a speeding greyhound. The drag remained untouched. The best way to break off a billfish is to tighten the drag, even slightly, when one is going away and jumping. The drag automatically increases slightly by itself as the reel empties of line and the spool must spin ever faster to let out each yard.

During those tense moments of the fight, surroundings began to fade away, leaving me the joyous solitude of combat between man and fish. The sounds of the crew, engines, waves against the hull, flapping of pennants, and the whistle of wind in the rigging and tower subsided. In its place comes the simple joy of pure combat. Big-game fishing relegates the problems, cares, and stresses of the everyday world to a far corner, to which we know we must return at some future time, but at least not for a while.

The fish was thrashing now on the surface—not exactly leaping, but with half its body out of water—shaking its head in an effort to throw the annoying hook from its jaw. The tremendous shock of those head shakes ran up the line, threatening to wrench my arms from their sockets.

Once again the fish leaped, but not so high as before, and then it sounded. The angle of the line began to slant downward, and the skipper put the controls into neutral. It was time to begin the slow, steady pumping motions, turning the reel handle only while lowering the rod, in order to get back line.

Down, down, and down dived the marlin. The drag steadily slipped at the strain, and the spool relentlessly continued turning. Finally the fish stopped. I could picture it in the darkness far below—its pectoral fins set in a diving angle much like the diving planes on a submarine. This fixed position of the fins on marlin make it a backbreaking task to pump the fish up. Several marlin have died at such depths, hooked from boats on which I have fished.

Now began the slow, rhythmic pumping necessary to get the head of the fish slanted slightly upward. For some time very little line was gained. After line was slowly recovered, dozens of yards would be lost suddenly when the fish made another short downward plunge. Finally we sensed, rather than knew, that the tide of battle was changing. The fish gave a few yards and slowly shook its head. Then, as the reeling became easier, the marlin began to come up slowly. The skipper eased his throttles into slow forward as he saw the angle of the line begin to change.

"He's coming up," the mate said from where he stood just behind the fighting chair. "Watch when he comes out!"

The angle of the line was changing rapidly now. The big fish had given up the idea of fighting it out in the depths and was heading for the surface. I was turning the reel handle as rapidly as possible to gain slack before the jump. Many hooks have been shaken loose by billfish that were given too much slack on weary but desperate jumps. They flail their heads from side to side, throwing the hook because there is no tension on the line to hold the barb in.

Out the marlin came, several hundred yards astern and slightly off to the port side. The leap did not carry his entire body out of the water, for he was tiring. The hook held as the fish thrashed from side to side, tearing the ocean surface into a white wake and flying spray. I was now gaining line rapidly.

"You want to keep him?" the skipper shouted.

This was a nice fish—somewhere between 300 and 400 pounds—but there seemed little reason to keep it. I shook my head. "OK," the skipper said. "We won't need the flying gaff or tail rope, John," he said to the mate. "You take the wire line and get ready to cut the leader after I tag him. If it's hooked in the throat or bleeding, let me know and we can boat it."

The mate nodded and moved to the stern at the port side to watch for the swivel, which would mark the end of the double line and the beginning of the wire leader. The marlin was coming in slowly now, with only an occasional burst of energy, but not thrusting more than half its length out of the water at any one time. The wallowing marlin never gave up, as tired as it was.

"Here's the swivel," said John, and he reached for it with a cloth-gloved hand. The skipper jumped down from the bridge with a plastic tag in his hand and leaned over the gunwale to clip it to the leading edge of the dorsal fin. When the mate had firmly taken the wire leader and was leading the marlin alongside, the drag was flipped to the free-spool position in case the fish, with a final spurt of energy, made a break for freedom. I have done this for years after seeing a Mexican skipper off Guaymas almost lose a foot.

"He's not bleeding, Cap'n," the mate said. "Hook is in the mouth."

The skipper nodded and fastened the tag to the dorsal fin, and John clipped the wire leader with a pair of fishing pliers. The hook would rust away shortly in the salt water. The marlin, swimming tiredly to freedom, sank slowly into the clear blue depths. My mind was refreshed and my body pleasantly tired after the struggle; it was time for a cold drink.

That total experience, for me, was billfishing at its best.

chapter five
The Bluefin Tuna

*I*t was the last day of the tournament and the Canadian team was leading with six fish. We, the eight members of the American team, had managed to land only three of the big "horse mackerel," and the weather on this, the last day, wasn't making life or the prospect of winning the annual tourney at Prince Edward Island any easier.

At 11:00 a.m., five miles out of the tiny port of North Lake, the rain was drenching us in the pitching 35-foot diesel-powered plank boat, and the four-to-five-foot seas were making life generally miserable even for seasoned big-game fishermen.

I was teamed up with Fred Archibald, a Florida big-game fisherman of no mean repute, who had lost a big bluefin the day before after four grueling hours in the chair. The American team had been hooked up seven times and had lost four fish in the past three days of the contest. We had been scheduled to compete four days, but the winds had been so high Wednesday that even the hardy commercial boats would not venture from the narrow harbor mouth into the massive, cold and gray August seas that pounded the entrance to the jetty. So it had turned into a three-day tournament, and this was to be the last day. The official quitting time, determined by our International Game Fish Association judges, was to be 4:30 p.m.; nothing hooked up later would count.

We were taking half-hour stints in the fighting chair and trying to heat the chill from our bones in the cabin between bouts with the downpour and seas. I had not gotten a strike in the tournament. For reasons known only to the patron saints of big-game fishermen, none of my partners the last two days had either. Boats all around us had been raising fish, losing fish and boating bluefins, but the boat on which I fished appeared to be jinxed. It was probably my imagination, but I sensed that the other team members were beginning to look at me strangely.

Fred lurched out of the chair and groped his way back to the cabin—his lips blue and hair plastered down by the cold rain.

"Your turn," he muttered, reaching for the offered hot black coffee and waving toward the crude chair. "I don't blame them for not hitting. They want to stay down there where it's warmer and drier."

My deep love for big-game fishing notwithstanding, I moved back toward the battered chair with no great enthusiasm. I had on the official tournament jacket over a heavy waterproof flotation jacket and several layers of wool sweaters and long underwear. The weatherbeaten plank fighting chair was a far cry from the plush and padded fighting chairs of the luxury sportfishermen used in the States. There was just the flat wooden chair seat, an ancient cracked leather-and-canvas kidney harness, and a welded steel footrest, probably resurrected from some discarded barber chair. The two reels were not exactly the latest—a battered, vintage Ocean City 14/0 and an old 12/0 Penn. But both were well cared for, and each held 800 yards of 130-pound braided nylon.

The mate helped snap the swivels to the big reel and to adjust the footrest to the proper length. After he had moved back to the shelter of the cabin roof, I hunched my shoulders, looked at my watch to verify the time and stared at the two "daisy chains" of rigged mackerel skipping astern in the sullen and gray sea. The # 13 hook was buried in the last bait on the chain. One chain of a half-dozen foot-long mackerel rode the swells on the starboard side approximately 30 feet back, skipping off to one side from a clip fastened to line from a 20-foot-long bamboo outrigger jutting out and up into a sodden sky. The other bait chain skittered as a flat line lure not more than 15 feet from the rough, salt-pitted transom of the aged boat. It bounced in the center of the churned wake—a practice no American big-game fisherman would try, most believing that the wake spooks fish.

There were several other tournament boats in sight on the horizon, and once we passed close to a big dory with two sou'wester-clad fishermen handlining strings of small mackerel over the gunwales. The red beaches and rolling green slopes of Prince Edward Island were barely visible off to our port side through the rain.

One moment there was nothing, and the next a wall of water pushed up into the tumbling white wake.

"Here he comes!" I heard the skipper shout, and automatically I reached for the rod in the right-hand holder as a tremendous explosion of water came over the transom and the bait chain disappeared into a vast cobalt-blue maw. I saw the dorsal fin and sickle-shaped tail as the big fish went under, and the reel shrieked as the line tore off the spool.

There is almost no way to describe the feeling of that much power packed into a big fish. The steel-tipped rod butt slammed into the seat gimbal and I leaned back, left hand clenched on the felt rod grip and my gloved right hand resting on the star drag. Hooking up to a bluefin feels like being fastened to a speeding train. There is nothing the angler can do on those first few runs but exert as much pressure on the fish as the tackle will stand. The sound of the reel was an ear-splitting scream by now, and the cockpit was full of action. The mate swung the old chair until he had me facing the direction of the streaking fish. Fred had jerked the line from the outrigger clip and was reeling the other bait string in as rapidly as possible to get it out of the way.

Three hundred yards of line had left the reel in a matter of seconds, and I eased the star drag on slightly.

"No, no!" The mate shouted in my right ear. "Don't give him any more. You'll break him off!"

I nodded but continued to add slightly more drag. Most big-game crews hate to see a fish lost, because the more they boat the better they look. But I always remember the voice of Bill Carpenter, president of the IGFA and a man who has caught more than a hundred bluefins in his life.

"Stop 'em or pop 'em," he said to me once at Cat Cay during the annual tuna tournament. He was standing with Annie Kunkel, the fine woman big-game angler who has caught more than a hundred bluefin tuna. She had nodded in agreement.

The first few runs of the big fish are the crucial ones. If the fish senses it has a chance, the fight will probably be a long one. If one can exert enough pressure in the first few dashes for freedom, psychologically, the fish will already have lost the battle — even though it may still take considerable time to get it in.

The harness was cutting into my back and the fingers of my left hand clenched tight as I lifted the rod and leaned back with all my strength, legs straight against the metal foot plate. The fish was taking a lot of punishment from the drag, the heavy, bowed fiberglass rod and the movement of the boat.

It seemed hours before the mate grunted and leaned close to my ear.

"He's stopping, he's slowing down," he said hoarsely. The reel spool was barely turning now.

I lowered the rod tip almost to the horizontal, took three or four quick turns of the reel handle and leaned back into the pull.

"He took more than 600 yards of line on that run," the mate said. His voice was a faint background sound.

Now, as always, came the sheer, pure joy of physical combat with the fish. Forgotten was the cold, slashing rain, the throbbing of the diesel engines and the gray seas dumping water into the cockpit. There was just the pumping of the big rod, the exhilaration of feeling the huge fish's head shake in anger and frustration; the cranking of the big reel handle and the pleasant ache of straining leg, back and arm muscles. But most of all, for me, there was the uncomplicated thrill of battling an adversary which had most of the advantages on its side—it being in its own element and much stronger than I, and I foreign and out of place in the big fish's world.

I found myself again in that special world where there are no grays—just black and white, win or lose. It is this simplified world, far removed from the confused one in which we all live each day, that keeps me big-game fishing.

The reel spool began to wail, for the third or fourth time. I added a fraction more drag and leaned back to let the heavy rod absorb the power of the fish. In a few moments the run slowed and the fish began to shake its head from side to side. It was in about sixty feet of water.

The shocks of the thrashing head traveled up the line, into the rod and into my left shoulder. With each shake the reel spool spun and the rod bent. And suddenly it was all over.

"He's off," I said quietly. The feel of the cold rain on my face returned.

"What?" the mate shouted.

I held the rod up and pointed to the tip. The big rod

was still bowed, but only from the weight of almost 700 yards of heavy line.

"Reel, reel!" the mate said. "Maybe he's coming toward the boat."

I shook my head. I felt the pitching of the boat and could smell the diesel fuel. I turned half in the chair and glanced at the captain over my right shoulder. "Full ahead, skipper," I shouted. "He's off, but let's make sure."

The captain nodded and the roar of the engines filled the cockpit. The angle of the line streaming astern changed slowly, but there was no more power on the other end—just dead weight. The skipper gradually slowed down, shifted into neutral, then reversed and began to back down as I started the long retrieve of line. Cranking in 700 yards of 130-pound line can be as difficult as bringing in a fair-sized amberjack or grouper. While the muscles of my right arm had not telegraphed the strain of the fighting fish, they protested against the work of bringing in the inert line.

"Fish broken off on the *Princess Anne*," was the voice of our IGFA judge speaking into the radio.

"Name of angler, please," came back the response from the tournament boat.

"Samson, American team."

"Right," came the answer. "Reason for loss?"

"We won't know for a bit. Line still coming in."

"Confirm time of hookup as 12:20 a.m., please."

"That's right," said our judge. "Breakoff time 12:46 p.m."

I glanced at my watch. It was 12:57. My God, where had that time gone?

The strain had lessened and the double line finally came over the transom. The mate ran the heavy line through his gnarled hand until he came to the break. It was where the double line had been fastened to the wire leader. "Damn," he said and shook his head. I unsnapped the swivels from the big reel and slid it back into the rod holder on the chair. I got up and walked to the shelter of the cabin roof as the mate began to rig up the line again. There was the taste of bile in my mouth, and fatigue washed over me.

"Broken at the double line," said the judge, a Canadian, into the radio. "Noted. Rotten luck. Our best to angler."

I nodded. Fred rested a hand on the shoulder of my soaked jacket.

"I know how you feel," he said simply. I thought of his four-hour ordeal the day before. He knew.

"Thanks," I said. "I could use a drink."

The skipper fished a flask from beneath the wheel and handed it to me. The brandy felt like scalding water as it went down — warming me almost instantly. The disappointment began to fade, as it always does.

"Well," I said to Fred, "there're still three and a half hours to go. Let's see you haul one of these monsters in."

He grinned, slapped me on the shoulder and made his way back to the chair. The mate and I helped him into the harness. I put out the other outrigger bait while the mate rigged up another bait chain for the flat line from the mackerel, which had been soaking in a pail of brine to keep them tough.

The rain let up an hour later and the wind began to die down as the afternoon wore on. We removed several layers of sweaters and ended up wearing just the light official jackets over long woolen underwear. We had both been in the chair several times, but there had been no action. Baitfish schools had churned up the surface of the sea in many areas as we trolled back and forth along the coast of the beautiful island. Several other boats were hooked up, but the fish were lost — one in a matter of minutes and another after almost two hours. One of our team members lost his after the reel handle came off and he fought it with a large nail inserted in the metal arm as an improvised handle. There was to be a victory and awards banquet starting at 7:00 p.m., and I had begun to think about a hot shower and a couple of drinks before dinner.

It was 3:50 — forty minutes before official quitting time — when the big bluefin smashed the bait chain behind the transom. The wall of water doused Fred in the chair and caught us by surprise. We had all been thinking of starting back, resigned to the loss of the one fish.

I jerked the line from the starboard outrigger and began pumping in the bait chain as Fred grabbed for the same rod I had before and hung on as the old reel began its wailing complaint again. The mate swung the chair as the huge fish headed north toward the cliffs about three miles away.

"Hookup on the *Princess Anne*," our judge shouted into the radio. "3:50 p.m., angler, Archibald, American team."

"Roger," came the answer. "Noted. Hell of a time to do that."

Fred leaned back and held the rod aloft, the big stick bowed against the afternoon sky.

"Tell that to this big bastard!" he laughed.

Fred was about six feet two inches tall, weighed close to 200 pounds, was in his early thirties and in excellent physical shape. I shook my head and went forward for a bottle of cold Alpine beer and a camera. Even if the fight went a little long, I thought as I reached into the ice chest, we would probably still be back in time for the dinner.

At 4:30—when the official tournament boat contacted all the competing boats to tell them the baits must be taken from the water and that the tournament was officially over except for those anglers fighting fish—the big bluefin was still out over 500 yards from us and still taking line when it felt like it. One other angler on the Canadian team was hooked up and had been for almost three hours.

Twenty minutes later the tournament boat came by and stood off several hundred yards as photographers from the local newspapers and television cameramen took still shots and some film footage. A short time later they wished us luck over the bullhorn and headed toward the harbor, visible down the coast.

At some time after 6:00 p.m.—with Fred stripped of his jacket and down to a woolen undershirt top—the

Canadian angler boated his tuna to make it a total of seven for their team. With only four boated for the American team, we couldn't win even if Fred succeeded in bringing this stubborn fish to gaff, but—in the spirit of big-game fishing—this had become unimportant now. It was the fish that mattered.

The sun dropped slowly toward the western horizon, and the surface of the sea had become glassy, with a burnished-bronze cast. I took some fine color pictures of Fred and the mate silhouetted against the sun, as the giant fish bored through the deep water—its great scimitar tail propelling it against the tide and its tremendous strength apparently undiminished. Just before dark a number of small boats came out from the harbor and drifted several hundred yards away from us. They were filled with townspeople watching the battle. They watched for almost an hour, then left—headed for the cluster of lights marking the harbor and jetty.

I got a flashlight from the forward locker and stood behind the mate, who continued to swing the chair in the direction of the fish. I played the light on the line so Fred could see the angle of line at all times. Several times we had the fish up close to the boat, but each time it came up under the transom on the port side, and the captain was forced to increase the power to keep the line from being cut by the propellers. At the same time he had to swing the bow to port to keep the fish from under the boat. And each time the double line and the wire leader would move back behind the boat and the big fish, having seen the boat, would begin another surging run.

Fred—now in the fifth hour of his fight—was drenched with sweat. His face was set in that expression big-game fishermen know so well—not fatigue as much as a combination of anguish and resolve. He had been operating on reserve energy for some time—after several cups of hot tea, a soggy sandwich and several beers had been handed to him.

The flashlight batteries began to lose power after 9:00 p.m. and the skipper radioed the dock for help. A boat was dispatched with a powerful flash which could be run off the boat batteries. It took the boat nearly half an hour to find us, and a youngster handed our judge the flash and cord over our bow, to prevent coming near the line and fighting fish. My arms had long ago gone numb from holding the flashlight on the rod tip and line, and my legs ached from constantly either standing behind the mate or walking around him as he swung the chair. I could imagine how Fred felt.

Sometime after 10:00 p.m. — the big fish had just made another incredible run and then had thrashed on the surface about 200 yards back in the darkness — Fred rested his forehead on his stiffened left elbow.

"Give up," he said, evenly, as if to himself. "Give up, damn you, give up." Then he raised his head, took a deep breath and began pumping the rod.

Around 11:00 p.m. the beer, sandwiches, coffee, tea and crackers were gone. A box of sugar cubes remained to give the big man in the chair an occasional surge of energy as the big fish continued to swim evenly through the black water. A slight wind began to come up and I asked the judge to put the heavy padded jacket on me — not daring to take the light from the line lest Fred lose sight of the all-important direction and angle.

We had drifted about a mile east of the harbor and were in fairly close to shore as the hands of my watch crept slowly around the hour of midnight and we entered into a new day. The fish had been under the boat several times and almost lost to the spinning propellers. It was a never-ending nightmare of pumping it close to the boat; sighting its huge, silver-blue image with the flashlight in the clear depths below and to the port side of the transom; watching it start to come up and then having to swing the boat and add power to keep it clear. I had long since ceased to feel any physical sense of fatigue, hunger, anxiety, thirst or anger at the stubborn fish. There was only the gleam of the white, braided line in the light beam, the labored breathing of the man with the heavy rod and the muttering of the diesel exhaust ports in the water at the stern.

A while later, the depth finder indicated 18 feet of water and Fred groaned.

"What's the bottom like?" he asked wearily.

"Sandy," the mate muttered. "Don't worry. Not many rocks."

I knew Fred was thinking the same thing I was. I could see the huge bluefin, nose-down at the bottom, trying to rub the leader on rocks. In spite of the shallow water—the boat was not more than a quarter-mile from the harbor entrance—the tuna continued to take out line on another run.

The big man braced his legs against the footrest, leaned back in the chair and hauled on the rod with what must have been a tremendous effort.

"Die, damn you," he said, as the reel spool continued to revolve slowly. "Give up you son of a bitch," he said through clenched teeth. "Give up, because . . ." He placed both hands on the rod. "Because I'm not going to. You hear me. I'm not."

I watched the angle of the line slowly change as the fish drew farther and farther from the boat.

And suddenly the reel slowed to a stop. I felt no emotion, nor, I think, did the mate or Fred. It was simply a fact.

The big man lowered the rod tip, took his right hand from the rod, took the reel handle and began to turn it. Slowly at first and just a little faster as time went on, he kept turning it. His breath was coming in gasps and he grunted with each long pump on the rod.

"He's coming in," the mate said. I nodded, knowing the mate was right and yet not really understanding how we knew.

I glanced at my watch. It was 1:40 a.m. The fish was out in the darkness about 300 yards away.

By 1:50 Fred had the fish less than 100 yards away. The steady pumping kept up and I could tell by a splash now and then that the bluefin was on or near the surface.

The mate looked at me. Then he turned to the captain.

"I'll clear the gaffs," he said slowly. "When I see the

double line I'll call out. Leave her in idle and take the long-handled gaff. I'll take the wire leader and try and sink the flying gaff at the same time. Keep the light on him at all times if you can," he said to me.

I nodded. The judge moved back into the cabin area to give us room.

"Double line," I said as the swivel gleamed in the blackness. Fred continued to pump, his breath a rasping sound in his throat.

Then there was the double line up close; the glint of shiny wire as the swivel came up.

The mate left the chair, reached down and picked up the flying gaff, reached out on the starboard side with a gloved hand and grasped the leader.

"Neutral, Skip," he shouted.

And there was the huge fish, coming up in shallow water—an immense torpedo of silver and dark blue, lying on its side. Its huge eye, as big as that of a horse, rolled in the light of the flash.

The mate reached out with one quick movement and sank the flying gaff into the back of the bluefin. With that the fish thrashed and hurled water over the entire boat. I tried to keep my footing but went down on the wet deck. I saw the skipper reach out with the second gaff and got to my feet in time to see him sink it into the silver underbelly. The fish began to thrash violently against the side of the thick hull.

Fred hurled himself from the chair and grabbed the rope of the flying gaff and braced his feet against the gunwale.

"Hold the light," I shouted to the judge, who took it from me as I grabbed the long-handled gaff from the captain. The fish almost tore my arms from the sockets.

"Get a meat hook into him, Skipper!" the mate shouted. "I'll try the tail rope."

The mate finally got the fish tail-roped, but not before the tuna almost broke his arm in the process. The captain had sunk another steel meathook into the back of the fish, passed a rope through its handle and fastened it to a cleat. He then passed a half-inch nylon line up

through the gill slits and out through the mouth of the still-thrashing giant tuna. It was not until he fastened that line to a forward cleat and the mate had tied the tail rope to the base of the fighting chair that I knew we had won.

I raised my head from the gunwale, where I was still clenching the wooden gaff handle and trying to keep bruised ribs from the rough gunwale wood.

Slowly Fred raised his head from between his arms, which were still straightened out, holding the thick rope of the flying gaff. He looked at me in the light of the flash and a grin slowly started to grow. "OK, lads," the mate laughed, "you can let go now. We got the mean, ugly son of a bitch!"

Fred let go of the rope and sprawled back in several inches of water on the cockpit deck. He started to laugh.

I sat down and leaned back against the cockpit. I thought I was too tired to laugh, but then I started to— and after that I couldn't stop.

And then it was handshakes and slaps on the back and falling down in the cockpit again and again as the crew and angler team, and the IGFA judge, joined in a wild victory dance on a wet plank boat gently rolling in the black water and darkness of a tiny harbor.

Even after the skipper had broken out his secret bottle of brandy he kept for special occasions and everyone had taken several large swallows, and the boat was halfway to the harbor, whose twinkling lights grew larger by the minute, the great fish continued to thrash, pounding over and over against the planks of the hull.

It had taken more than eleven hours to subdue the bluefin. It wasn't even a record fish, nor that huge a tuna either. The Canadians' biggest had weighed 788 pounds, and this stubborn young "green" bluefin finally weighed in at 655 pounds. But this fish was probably between ten and fourteen years old, in the prime of its life, and far stronger than some in the 1,000-pound class.

The banquet had been over long ago and the competing teams—after drinking up most of the beer and liquor of the tuna club at the harbor—came weaving down to the weighing dock to greet us as we eased into the slip. It was 3:00 a.m. before we had the fish hoisted on the towering iron scales, and even then the strong fish thrashed as it was being hauled tail-first up the concrete launching ramp.

Gone was the fatigue, the hunger, the cold, and the dampness. And in their place was the quiet, triumphant glow that comes with winning the battle with huge ocean fish. Between Fred and me there was only a simple handshake and a drink in salute. But that was enough.

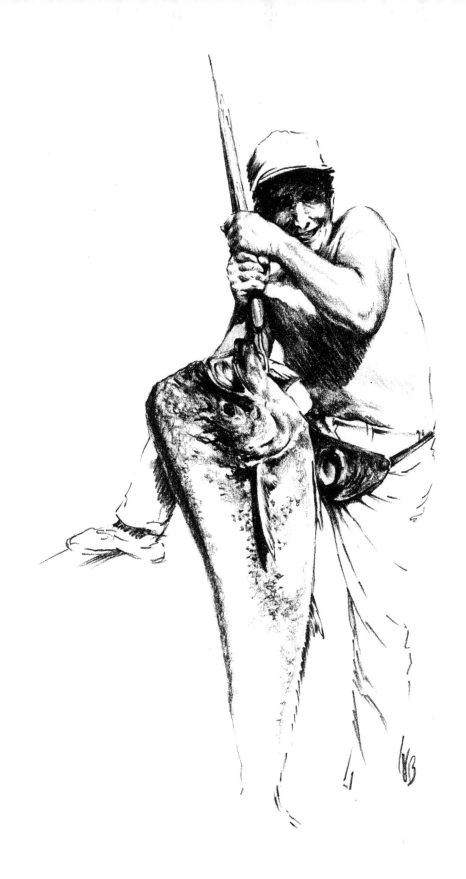

chapter six

The Dolphin

My oldest son, John, grabbed the spinning rod from the holder as the line dropped from the port outrigger and his reel began to sing.

Leaving the 85-horse outboard in slow forward speed, I swung the 17-foot boat to give him room to play his fish. I yelled "Line down!" and another son, Donald, popped out from the small cutty cabin where he had gone to get a cold drink. Donald, then thirteen, usually acted as skipper when we were trolling and had been until just a moment before.

He grabbed the wheel as I reached out and took the other rod from the holder and began reeling in line as fast as I could, the rigged balao bait skipping across the tops of the Gulf Steam waves about fifteen miles off the Florida coast.

"Dolphin!" Johnnie yelled as a nice fish broke the

surface about 50 yards back and sliced across the surface in a series of quick leaps.

"Keep your rod tip up," I cautioned as the speeding fish took out another 50 yards or so of his 17-pound-test monofilament line. It really wasn't necessary; the boy already had the tip high and was checking his drag with his left hand. Having caught saltwater game fish since he was a little boy in Cape May, New Jersey, he knew the ropes as well as I did.

I reeled the starboard balao bait until it was just below the outrigger and hung about a foot above the surface, then I jerked it from the clip on the outrigger line and reeled the bait aboard.

"Okay, John," I said, "the lines are in. This fish may go about 15 pounds."

He nodded, grimly playing the fighting fish.

I shoved the rod butt into the holder behind the console seat and took the wheel from Don.

"Buddy," I said, "hand me that light spinning outfit on the bunk, will you? You know how dolphin are. When Johnnie gets this one in close we can flip a lure out there and pick up another one. The school should stay around until he boats his. Put on a silver spoon or anything that flashes."

He nodded and ducked into the cabin again.

I turned to watch the water and slipped the throttle into neutral. The boy didn't need any help, and I glanced toward the distant shoreline of Ft. Lauderdale, slightly hazy in the afternoon sunlight. The seas were running about two to three feet where we were, and the water of the Stream was a deep, royal blue as it flowed northward at about six miles per hour.

"I got him, Dad," John said, pumping his fish alongside where I could see the incredible gold, silver, green and blue colors of the world's most beautiful gamefish.

"He's not too big. I can gaff him by myself." He reached for the short gaff stored in the port gunwale. "There's a whole school of them down there, Dad."

I leaned over and peered into the cabin.

"You got the spinning rod, Don?" I asked.

The boy looked up from where he was sitting on the bunk, the tackle box between his feet.

"I'm putting a bigger swivel on the line," he answered. "Just a minute."

John reached over to gaff his fish and I knew it would be too late to take any of the others in a moment.

I knew I couldn't cast the bait with the larger boat rod that had the 9/0 reel on it, but I figured if I got a balao bait back there I might take another fish.

Slipping the throttle into forward, I reached out and took the rod from the holder and dropped the balao over the side. The rig had a #7 hook at the end of about fifteen feet of stainless-steel leader. I flipped the lever and free-spooled the bait back behind the boat where it sank slowly in the clear water.

I engaged the drag lever and jerked the bait a couple of times. A streaking fish struck at it and the balao flew out of the water. Behind it was a small dolphin, apparently having just taken a small bite out of the bait. The balao fell back and I let it sink, planning on jigging it a few more times.

Before I could do anything, though, I saw a flash as a fish took the bait, and the line tightened. Thinking it was the same 8- or 10-pounder, I raised the rod tip a little and set the hook fairly easily, not wanting to pull the hook out of the small fish with 20-pound mono.

The strike almost tore the rod from my hands. I was sitting on the console seat and was holding the rod at an angle 90 degrees laterally from where the fish was. Don came up from the cabin at that very moment, the light spinning rod in his hand. John had just slid his small dolphin over the gunwale when the surface of the Gulf Steam 20 feet behind the boat burst open as though somebody had rolled a depth charge over the stern. A great gold, silver and green monster with a head that looked as big as a whale's thrashed up out of the water, trying to rid itself of the hook.

"Holy cow!" Donnie shouted as the huge bull dolphin fell back to the surface, spraying water over the boat. "A 50-pound dolphin!"

The boy didn't know how close he was to guessing the weight of that fish. He later said he just picked the largest round number he thought possible for a dolphin.

I was too busy to worry about the weight. A dolphin—pound for pound—is one of the toughest fish to boat. Its flat sides give it a tremendous advantage when it turns sideways to the angler and either bores for depth or streaks for distance.

Fortunately I had the drag set light, having been trolling for sailfish, and I scrambled for the portable fighting chair. The reel screamed as 100 yards left the spool in a matter of seconds.

"Give me about quarter-speed," I shouted at Don, who stowed the spinning rod and leaped behind the wheel. "Watch my line and follow him."

I glanced down at the spool as the boy added power and the sleek boat picked up speed, a white wake boiling astern. John was stowing loose gear and sliding the top over the fish box. The night before I had wound 400 yards of new 20-pound line on the reel. I had about 200 yards out already and had no intention of increasing the drag much more with that giant of a fish on such light line.

I squinted to starboard where my line was cutting the surface 50 yards out and muttered something to myself as old as the contest between man and fish. I would need luck with this one.

We really hadn't been fishing for dolphin at all, although saltwater gamefishermen expect to pick one up at any time and look forward to it. They are great fighters and my favorite eating fish.

The week before we had entered our boat in the annual billfish tourney at Ft. Lauderdale—a tournament which attracts several hundred boats each year and which usually sees fine September weather.

This year a cold front had moved into the Middle Atlantic States and had pushed down to northern Florida. This, combined with a low pressure area, brought gale winds and driving rain to southeastern Florida and had forced the cancellation of the three-day tourney the previous weekend.

The wind had kept up most of the week and on Friday, the day before, the Coast Guard had not held out much hope for good weather. Most of the boats in the tournament were sportfishermen in the 31- to 55-foot class and even they had no plans to tackle the sloppy seas of the Stream.

Yet late Friday night the winds slacked off and Saturday morning the seas were running two to three feet close to shore and three to five feet in the Gulf Stream. The bad weather had pushed the clear blue water of the Stream far from shore and it was more than ten miles out before we left the light-green sandy water churned up by the violence of the past week and hit the beautiful blue of the Stream.

We had left with the annual "Bimini start"—all the contesting boats lined up along the beach heading for the Gulf Stream at the starting signal. With an 85 horse outboard on a 17-foot double-hulled planing boat we had the satisfaction of leaving practically every bigger and more luxurious sportfisherman far behind in the race for the fishing grounds.

Once there, however, we sacrificed air-conditioning and considerable space in the cockpit for the mobility of a small boat. But we were outrigged well—even carried kites for live-bait fishing—had a good big baitbox molded into the hull, excellent tackle, and most important of all, we knew our boat and operated well as a crew. We had started training in the grim and cold seas years before with a 17-foot plywood, lapstrake-hulled outboard boat off the New Jersey coast, and the Florida Gulf Stream was heaven to us after the bitter winds and seas of early spring and later fall in the Atlantic to the north.

The boys knew charts, weather, and navigation, and we carried every safety device required by the Coast Guard—plus a number we always added, such as a small auxiliary motor stowed in the bow, extra rations, fresh water, and foul-weather clothing.

Nevertheless, there had been some snickers when the boys and I checked in at the committee boat prior to the start of the tourney.

There were a few mentions of fishing from a dinghy, and a couple of salty skippers and mates—probably many who had never seen a cold sullen rip off Cape Hatteras or Montauk in late fall—wondered aloud where we would put a billfish if we caught one.

The boys took it well—with grins—as we got the "go" sign for our boat, number 120. A lot of good fish have come aboard our small boats, and John, then fifteen, already had more saltwater game fish to his credit than most adult deep-sea anglers.

We trolled fruitlessly back and forth for hours, keeping just off the green water and blue water separation line. We were dragging one rigged balao bait and a small mullet—primarily fishing both for sailfish and white marlin. I was also prepared for a blue marlin at any time and hoped that if one did hit, it would be on the 20-pound rather than the 12-pound line on the spinning reel.

The last blue marlin I had had on had battled me for eight and a half hours on 12-pound line and I lost it to a shark just behind the transom by moonlight off North Key Largo. That heartbreaker had qualified me as a candidate for the Philip Wylie Hard Luck Trophy in the Greater Miami Tournament a few years back.

Shortly after noon I ran a fishing kite up and used it as an auxiliary outrigger—skipping a balao bait 50 yards out to starboard and about 50 yards astern. Even that didn't bring them up. We didn't know then that only four sails were to be taken that day by the almost 100 boats out. Apparently the bad weather had put them down and they had not begun to feed yet.

It was almost two o'clock when John took his small dolphin and suddenly all thoughts of billfish were put aside as I settled down to fight a giant dolphin I wasn't at all certain of landing. I wasn't concerned about the test strength of the line, as I usually fish with light tackle and have encouraged the boys to do the same. We find it much more fun than wearing down great fighting fish with 80- or 130-pound line. We lose a lot of fish, but the ones we catch are fish of which we can be proud.

I was concerned about getting this monster aboard. Boating billfish, to my mind, is far easier than trying to land a dolphin—especially a big one. A billfish, when it finally tires, can be taken by grabbing the bill with gloved hands and whacking it between the eyes with a short bat. After that it is simply a matter of slipping a noose over its tail and then hauling it aboard by holding onto both ends. With a dolphin of this size, there was only one thing to do, and that was to sink a gaff into it and hope it would hold long enough to get it over the side. John was big for his age, but he weighed only about 130 pounds. That is asking a lot from a boy.

Taking the wire leader in a gloved hand wouldn't do any good, since this fish could easily break a leader, and we don't carry a flying gaff aboard.

"Slow it down, Don," I shouted over the engine noise. "I'm gaining line on him." The fish, not having solved his problem by the several-hundred-yard run, decided to try depth.

Don swung the boat in a wide circle, watching the direction of my line, and eased back on the throttle as the angle of the line slanted down.

"That's the way, Skipper," I grunted as the big fish began shaking its head in the depths. I had shoved the rod butt into the gimbal of the folding fighting chair, and my arms were beginning to feel the battle. I weigh 175 pounds and keep in fair shape, but this fish was far more in his element than I was.

I always wear a leather Bimini belt while fishing big-game fish and have found many times that it really pays—especially if one has to get up quickly and battle a fish which is in danger of passing under the boat or is coming in to the gaff.

"What time is it, John?" I asked, wiping the sweat from my eyes. "Two-thirty, Dad," John said from his position in the stern, where he stood holding the big gaff. "He's been on for nearly 45 minutes."

"Douse me, will you?" I said.

John slid the gaff inside the gunwale and dipped a small blue plastic bucket over the side. He poured the contents over my head and shoulders and grinned as I sputtered. It's a good trick and really feels welcome when a stubborn fish is not doing much.

"He's coming up," Donnie shouted from behind me. He was right. I started taking in line as fast as I could as the angle of the line slanted up.

Don eased the throttle open slightly to give me less slack and swung the bow away from the direction of the fish.

"There he is!" John yelled as the great fish burst from the water about 125 yards astern and shook its head violently in the bright sunlight.

The fish jumped twice more, each time shaking its head so violently I wondered how the hook stayed in. But after that the battle settled down to a brutal contest of gaining and losing line, while I watched the drag very carefully to see that the big fish didn't catch me off guard with a sudden run.

It was about three-fifteen when the huge fish came alongside. It was getting tired, but it wasn't licked. My arms felt like lead.

"Turn the motor off, Don," I said. "And Johnnie, raise the engine. I don't want him lost in the prop if he makes a run under the boat. Besides, we don't need the power any more."

John nodded, stowed the gaff, and heaved on the big motor until the lock snapped in place.

"Holy cow," Don said again, staring down into the depths where the big fish was slowly circling. "What a fish! How we going to get him in, Dad?" he asked.

I looked at the leader. It was about fifteen feet long. That, plus the length of the six-and-a-half-foot fiberglass rod, was as close as I was going to get to this fish. Either John was going to have to try to gaff it alone or I was going to have to try it while holding the rod, because if I handed the rod to one of the boys while I gaffed the fish, I couldn't enter the dolphin in competition.

"I don't really know, Don," I said, bringing the fish to the surface where it lay on its side close to the starboard stern, weaving slowly.

"John?" I asked, looking at the boy. He stared at the fish, looked at me and at the gaff in his hands. He nodded slowly.

Then I made up my mind.

"Listen," I said quickly, "I think I can gaff him myself. It's not that you couldn't do it, John, but if you miss him and he gets away you are going to feel much worse about it than I am. If I miss, I'll have nobody to blame but me. OK?"

He stood quietly for a minute, then silently nodded. I could see the relief on his face.

"OK," I said, "clear the cockpit." I looped the leather thong of the long gaff around my right wrist and then reeled until the swivel connecting the line to the wire leader was right at the top guide of the rod. Then I slowly raised the rod with my left arm, the butt end stuck in the leather belt socket. The big fish swung in close to the boat, and its dorsal fin broke the clear water.

Because it was vertical in the water I couldn't get a clear swipe at the underjaw or belly with the gaff and would have to settle for the hard head or back. I knew if I hit it too far back, it would have a lot of diving power once it got its head down, so I gambled on the top of the big forehead and, reaching far out, jerked down and toward me. The point struck hard gristle but held. The shock momentarily stunned the big fish, and for a second it did not thrash. I dropped the rod, propped my left foot on the gunwale, and hauled with all my strength.

The huge head slid over the white fiberglass gunwale, the gaff pulled out, and I fell backward across the

boat. For what seemed an eternal second the fish tee-
tered on the edge, then suddenly slithered forward and
crashed to the floor of the cockpit.

A styrofoam baitbox—used to keep rigged balao
and mullet on ice—was stowed in a corner. It was reduced to white powder in a matter of seconds as the fish
pounded everything in sight with its tail.

I took a swipe across the right arm which stayed
black and blue for two weeks. John, trying to locate our
billfish club, almost suffered a broken ankle in the melee. I sank the gaff into the back of the dolphin and tried
to yank him upright so we could clobber him with the
club before he demolished the boat. I got his head up
and John—with all his might—smashed the three foot
sawed-off oar handle across the dolphin's forehead. The
oar handle broke in half, but the huge fish quivered and
died, its fantasy of colors slowly fading.

I didn't realize I was so exhausted until I let go of
the gaff handle and looked at my hands, which were
shaking from exertion. I sat down on the gunwale and
hung on.

Donald, who had been shouting advice, warnings,
and encouragement from the pilot's seat during the
whole battle, climbed down in awe to touch the fish.

"Whew," said John and also found a seat. "Thanks
for not letting me gaff him, Dad," he said. "I'd never
have made it."

"Forget it." I laughed shakily. "Nobody will ever
come closer to losing a fish than I just did." I got to my
feet with an effort and grabbed the bucket. "Let's wash
everything down and get this guy to shore before he
dehydrates. We may have a world record here."

So that was it. We didn't have a world record, but
we did have a dolphin weighing 47½ pounds, and that
is just a few pounds off the world record—especially on
20-pound line.

The experts who joked about dinghies and where
we would put a big fish were mysteriously absent at the
weighing dock. But the dolphin took the biggest non-
billfish prize of the tourney, and the four sailfish that

came in that day weighed 44 pounds, 47 pounds, 42 pounds, and 39 pounds. The dolphin beat them all.

It confirmed what we already knew: It's not the size of the boat that matters. Even more important—to me, anyway—it proved that what really counts isn't the boat at all, but the way the crew acts as a team when a big fish gets on the line.

chapter seven
The Special World . . .

We were kite fishing with Captain Allen Self out of North Key Largo aboard the 31-foot *Sea Elf*, and it was a perfect spring day for blue-water fishing—the hot sun pouring down on the dazzling white gunwales and cockpit of the idling, compact sportfisherman.

I had fished with Allen a number of times. I consider him one of the true pioneers in the kite-fishing field. While it is true that Tommy Gifford, Johnnie Harms and Bob Lewis, among others, did much to promote the sport of kite fishing in America, Allen Self—more than any other skipper I know—sticks to this type of big-game fishing almost exclusively. Allen has refined kite fishing to the point of using helium-filled balloons to keep his kites aloft when the winds die down and the sea becomes calm. He averages 100 billfish a year off his home port.

He was using a balloon today, a large orange one he had filled from his compressed-helium cylinder. He had run out two lines—both 20-pound mono on 9/0 reels, one at 100 feet out and the other fastened to a second clip at 50 feet out. The slight breeze blew from the southeast and the two lines dropped to the surface of the royal-blue Gulf Stream water as we drifted northward toward Biscayne Bay. The more distant line was baited with a blue runner, hooked lightly through the flesh of the back with a #7 hook. The inboard bait was a pilchard, hooked the same way and on the same-size hook. Allen stood by the port gunwale, where he could work his remote controls to the twin engines and also keep a hand on the kite reel, keeping the swimming baits just below the surface.

We had taken a double on dolphin just before noon, Larry and I—one 26 pounds and the other close to 30—lines crossing and fish slicing across the surface behind the boat. We boated both. Then his wife Claudia, a fine fisherman, brought in a 61-pound sail after thirty minutes. When the mate took it by the bill she leaned over the side. "Let it go," she said.

"It's bleeding," the mate said. "It probably wouldn't get far—the sharks . . ." She thought a moment, then nodded. The sail came aboard, glistening in the bright sunlight. We went back to fishing, and had beer and sandwiches.

It was 1:25 in the afternoon when the marlin showed close to the bait.

"Billfish!" was all the captain shouted from above. I reached out and took the rod and fitted the rod handle into the leather belt socket.

"Line down!" the captain shouted. The fish had struck, and the line had been plucked from the clip of the outrigger line. When the fish had had enough time, having taken up the slack, I struck it. Nothing happened. I raised the rod tip higher and began to pump the rod slowly, reeling steadily. There was pressure on the line.

The first leap caught me by surprise. Fortunately I kept the tip on the fiberglass rod high as the fish went up about 10 feet and fell back with a tremendous splash. I backed into the chair and jammed the rod handle into the seat socket as the fish came out again 50 feet or so out from the boat and headed toward shore 10 miles away.

"Yeoowwww!" the mate screamed. "Marlin! Jesus, look at him go!"

The golden reel on the throbbing rod whined as the light line was stripped from it. The fish began a series of straight jumps—none of them high—and headed for the big red buoy about a quarter of a mile off our starboard bow, crashing through the low chop each time it came down.

I don't know how many times the fish jumped. Later they told me perhaps as many as twenty.

I had 600 yards of line, and the fish had run about 400, leaving precious little on the spool. Suddenly the fish came out of the water and fell back to the surface in a shower of white spray. Claudia gasped. "My God," she said, "how beautiful."

"I don't think it's a white," Larry said. "I think it's a blue." Whites this size broke records; among blues my fish would not be unusual.

But the mate said, "I think it's a big white. No blues taken off Largo this season so far."

"I don't know," Larry said. "It sure looked like a blue when it jumped the first time."

I settled down to my business. The line had been pretested at 20 pounds, but it had been on the reel for more than three weeks, during which time it had taken a number of sails and little white marlin. All this meant that the wet breaking test now was probably around 14 pounds. I would have to be very careful not to increase the drag too much. From what I had seen of the fish on its first jump up close, the marlin might weigh 200 pounds. It appeared to be about eight feet long, and it looked like a blue. I had to be careful of the jumps—not to let the fish have enough slack while in the air to shake out the hook, and not to let it gain too much slack by coming at the boat. I eased back in the chair.

"What kind of a marlin do you think it is, Skipper?" Larry asked.

Allen—nearing sixty years, forty of them in charter-boat fishing—shook his head slowly. His weathered forehead creased as he frowned. "I really don't know. It could be a white. I was pretty busy with the boat. It looked more like a small blue to me."

I nodded. "What time is it, Captain?" I asked. "Two-nineteen," he said.

That had been a fast half-hour. I slowly took the cork grip in my right hand, and let go with my left hand for the first time. I flexed the fingers of my left hand. I had trouble straightening them out.

"Damn!" the mate said. He was about twenty-five, with blond hair bleached white from the Florida sun. "If this really is a white it will be something."

The captain grunted. "Better boat it first," he said.

Twenty minutes passed; I raised the rod tip and began reeling slightly faster.

"He's coming in," I said. "He couldn't be tired yet." I glanced at the captain.

The fish came up rapidly behind the stern—not too deep—and I took up the line until I could feel the slight vibration of the current. The fish was just back of the stern on the starboard side. I had seen marlin quit after thirty minutes for no apparent reason. Maybe he was hooked in the throat and the bleeding had tired him.

The mate reached out slowly. He grasped the leader and led the fish closer to the boat. He looked down into the prismatic sea and slowly waved his free left hand behind him.

"A little forward, Skipper," he shouted. "Keep him away from the screws." I felt the boat surge forward a little as the captain added power. The line began to slip slowly through the gloved fingers and suddenly the mate let go and nodded at me.

"Take him again," he said. "It's a blue." I kept the

tip up and suddenly the marlin began another series of jumps, thrashing its head and bill as it churned across the choppy surface. The reel shrieked as the line stripped off. "I think he just came in to look at us."

"The fish is foul-hooked," the mate said, his tone sympathetic. "I guess when it took a swipe at the bait the hook caught in the leading edge of the dorsal fin. That's a solid hooking spot. I could see it real clear in the water. So you're not hurting him with a hook in the mouth or throat, not at all."

I reeled slowly, not gaining on the diving fish. It might not even feel the steady pressure of the rod and the resistance of the line. The marlin was slowly pumping downward.

"It's a fine fish," Claudia said.

Larry said nothing.

I swung the chair around and looked at the captain. "What about a flying gaff?"

"Don't have one aboard," he said.

There was no reason he should. Most of the whites taken off the Keys were in the 50-to-70 pound class. An ordinary gaff would do on them.

"Any boat close by carry one?"

The captain nodded. "The *Semper Fi* has one. She's a few miles off. Let's raise her and see if they won't come by and drop one off."

The mate climbed the ladder to the bridge and headed for the radio. I went back to concentrating on the fish. By the time I got it close—or the time after that—they might have a flying gaff ready. The hook and line of a flying gaff disengage from the pole after the barb is set. With it the mate can handle the fish with greater control and land it sooner.

The marlin was still going down.

This was no classic *Old Man of the Sea* battle. I was not miles at sea in a dory, as was the old man in his famous story, nor was I using a hand line. I was just a man who loved to fish, and who was getting a lot of it.

After a while the mate climbed back down the ladder. He moved up to the captain.

"The radio cuts in and out," he said. "Can't carry on a conversation."

"Check the battery-terminal connection?"

The mate removed the engine hatch and climbed down. He climbed out a moment later.

"Seems okay."

"Damn," the captain said. "What a time for it to act up. Must be a tube."

The mate nodded and moved over to the gunwale and sat down. I shifted my right hand to the rod again and looked at Larry leaning against the ladder.

"Anything against drinking a beer?"

He smiled and opened the ice chest. He popped the top of the can and placed it close to me on the gunwale.

"Looks like I'm going to spoil your afternoon's fishing," I said.

"Maybe it will be worth it," he said quietly, keeping my beer can from sliding as the boat rolled with a swell.

There was nothing to do now except apply enough pressure to make it as difficult as possible for the marlin to dive and yet not break the line. I shifted in the seat and then stood up. "I'm tired of the chair." I stuck the rod handle into the leather belt socket and braced myself against the transom. "I'm going to try to work him up," I said. Allen nodded.

Claudia had gone up forward and was sitting in a chair in the cabin. She had picked up a magazine. Larry had lowered himself into a folding chair, with a beer, and was staring out at the faint outline of the Keys on the horizon to the west. It was 3:55. The wind was clean and sweet over the Gulf Stream. There was the steady pressure of the marlin, fathoms below, pumping for the bottom—fighting something it did not understand. There was the tilting horizon, the slow passage of a freighter, hull down, with a plume of smoke blowing back from one stack. There was the warmth of the sun on my back, shoulders, and the back of my thighs. My arm muscles had long ceased to ache.

My attention would be preoccupied for minutes by a

bit of seaweed drifting, the yellow of the weed against the blue depths. There was a man-o'-war bird overhead, circling. Gradually everything was reduced to the basic: There was the fish on one side, I on the other, and the great, clean sea lay between. I was faced with the utter simplicity of a fish I could not control.

At 4:38 I brought the fish alongside. The mate grasped the leader, could not maneuver the weight, and had to let go. The fish jumped three times and sounded.

At 5:20 I brought the fish alongside again—under the stern at the starboard side. The mate again grasped the leader, brought the fish up to within two feet of the surface, and then, feeling it turn its side toward the current, let go of the leader again.

About 6:00 p.m. the captain, after a long discussion with me, advised that I might increase the drag some— not enough to break the line but perhaps enough to make a slight difference in tiring the fish.

I advanced the drag and was able to bring the fish alongside twice more in the next half-hour, but always on the starboard stern—the wrong angle for the mate to try to grasp the bill and allow me to turn it over to him. Each time the fish was able to move away.

It was between 6:00 and 6:30, I believe, when the captain stood beside me watching the line slanting back 200 yards to where the marlin had just wallowed on the surface for a few moments—appearing as fresh as five hours earlier. He coughed and looked at me carefully. "You say what you want. It's a good fish. I'll stay as long as you want."

The sun was low on the horizon and the seas were up a little. The wind had freshened and, with no shirt on, I was feeling the chill. I looked at him and then went back to the fish.

"I'll stay," I said.

"Good," he said gruffly, and went back to his throttles. The sun dropped. Then the full moon came up out of the sea. There were times when I thought the fish was weakening and brought it close to the boat, only to have it move out and down again. I really believe it was weakening—thinking back on it now—but it was difficult to tell at the time.

By 7:30 the darkness had begun to set in and the mate brought out a flashlight. He held it so that I could see the line and could judge the direction of the fish.

The sandwiches were gone, the beer had been disposed of hours before, the wind was whipping, and the seas were higher. The captain estimated that we had drifted more than 20 miles north of North Key Largo on the Gulf Stream. The climbing moon made a silver path on the irregular surface of the sea behind the boat, and occasionally the marlin would surface and break the silver band with a black, jagged tear of energy.

It was probably about 7:45 when I sensed the fish was defeated. Closer and closer it came and this time I began to believe that I was going to be able to bring it along the port side at the stern, giving the mate a good chance to grasp the bill.

Larry moved up close to me as I began to talk to the mate. He had another flashlight and played it on the black water. The line came in slowly, until I suddenly saw the brass swivel again. The mate leaned over the side, grasped the leader, and nodded his head when Larry switched the light over to the other side of the stern.

"My God," he said. "Look at the size of that shark!"

We saw the huge, tan-colored fish as it passed below the stern, and suddenly there was a sharp jolt on the line and it went slack.

The mate flipped the leader into the boat and ran the line up through his glove. The stainless-steel hook lay in the palm of his hand. On the tip of the hook was a chunk of white flesh with a fleck of gray skin.

"What happened?" Larry asked.

"I don't know," I said numbly. "There was a jolt and then the hook came free."

"The shark took him," the mate said, shaking his head and fingering the bright hook. He took off the small piece of meat and flipped it over the side.

The four of us stood looking at the black water boiling beneath the stern.

I glanced at the captain's watch close to my right hand. It was 8:05 p.m. I shoved the rod in the holder of the gunwale and rubbed my mouth with the back of one hand.

"I wish it hadn't been a shark," I said. "That was too good a fish."

Nobody said anything. Claudia was standing a few feet behind us.

"Well," Allen said, "we had better get started back. It's going to be a rough ride over the reef." I nodded and moved toward the cabin to get a sweatshirt.

"It was a . . ." Allen paused. "It was a damn good fight."

The mate nodded. "The hook just finally pulled out," he said. "Maybe the shark didn't even touch him. He couldn't have been bleeding, hooked in the dorsal the way he was."

The captain smiled and nodded. He began to climb the ladder to the bridge. The mate followed him and I felt the engines speed up as we began the long run for the marina.

Larry dug out a bottle of scotch he kept in a camera case, handed Claudia and me glasses and took one himself, and we all settled in chairs as the cruiser slammed into the seas on its way in.

We seemed to be running up a long runway of silver, the ribbon of moonlight stretched behind us to the horizon.

Claudia was silent, lost in thought. Larry, balancing his glass in the lurching cabin, stared at the silver sea behind us.

And in my mind, I could see the marlin, miles away, swimming slowly, tiredly toward the depths of the Gulf Stream.

chapter eight
A Green Fish

Mike Pritchard was a barrel of a man, about as black as a black man can get, and round and hard as a weathered wooden keg. He was a first-class charterboat skipper—born in Bimini and having served as a mate and finally skipper on fishing boats from West End to Eleuthera.

Mike ran a beautiful 45-foot wooden Mead sport-fisherman. The boat belonged to some wealthy Bahamian who lived in Nassau. He only used her a few times a year himself and the rest of the time let Mike use her for charter on a percentage basis.

The boat had twin diesel engines and was fully out-rigged. She had CB radio, depth finders and tower high enough to spot the most distant tuna school in the

spring. She was a thing of beauty, and Mike would run his hands over the scrubbed teak decks the way a quail hunter would fondle the walnut stock of a favorite old 20-gauge he'd had for decades.

The big Mead boat had taken many a tuna and marlin. But this morning, as I stood at the window of the cottage, I knew this was not going to be a good day. The wind was blowing about thirty knots out of the west—a sure sign that it would shift to the north by late in the day. As any Gulf Stream sailor knows, when the wind is against the prevailing northward drift of the Stream, it means trouble.

I was mentally calculating how many cases of beer we had on hand to keep Mike, me, Lucas and Basil alive for about seven hours on the rolling Stream.

I wasn't counting the customer from Miami. He could damn well fend for himself.

Lucas, for all his bitching about whites, and talk of a Bahamian revolution, was a first-class fishing mate. He was gentle with the baits and had good eyes for strikes. Also, he could land a fish with a minimum of strain and dispatch it with ease, without excessive blood and wrestling. At least he had done so in the past.

Basil, a huge Andros Island man, liked to go along because he loved the sea. He was good at any sort of work on a boat and was a reserve of immense strength in case of any emergency. He also drank very little beer, even though he ate most of the lunches packed for the rest of the crew.

As I dressed, I hoped Mike had found some malfunction in one of the diesel engines, but deep down I knew he would be ready to go. I always went when Mike invited me. I threw a tarp over two cases of beer, and took my favorite marlin rod from the closet—complete with the well-used reel—and slipped it into the uprights of the golf cart.

The harbor was calm, being in the lee of the island. Mike was on the bridge with a cup in his hand and lounged over the wheel as I ran the golf cart alongside the boat and pointed to the tarp. Big Mike waved Basil to the cart. The big man grinned and tucked the two cases underneath one arm, along with the tarp.

The man from Miami, today's customer, sauntered down the pier from where he had been talking to the customs agent close to a big yacht.

"Good morning, good morning," he boomed jovially, his face a little flushed—either from the night before or a bit of a nip with the morning coffee. He was wearing a fishing jacket with club emblems from half the world sewed to it. I handed the cart key to the dock master and told him to keep it safe. The customer climbed on board and headed for the galley, where Lucas was seated at a table scowling at his coffee.

"Hi," I said, reaching for a cup of coffee and sliding into the seat across from the mate. "What does it look like?"

"Bad," Lucas said, still scowling. "The goddam sea will be eight to twelve feet out there."

I sipped the coffee and shuddered at the taste.

"Stay home, man," I suggested. "We have Basil to run the lines."

"Basil!" Lucas exploded. "You want a tuna loaded aboard, mon, he great. You want a fisherman, forget it."

I sipped the acidlike coffee and felt my stomach wrench.

The customer slid down the companionway and looked at us. "Any chance for some coffee?" he asked casually. "Got to put some blood back in the old veins."

Lucas waved at the galley stove. "Help yourself," he said. "We got plenty to spare." I got up and headed for the bridge as I saw the poor guy pale at the first swallow.

"Let's go, Mike," I yelled at the bridge. Mike dislodged a leg from the wheel.

"Cast off the lines," Mike shouted at Basil, who tossed the spring line to the dockmaster while I got the stern lines off. Another dockhand had taken care of the bow line, and the Mead purred into the slot between the docks. I stuck my rod in a gunwale holder and climbed up to the bridge. I zipped up my preserver jacket against the light rain and looked at Mike.

"What you think?" I asked.

Mike spun the wheel to miss a yacht stern and grunted.

"Gonna be a bitch out there, mon," he said. "But you got paying customers—you got big wheels."

"Why don't you call it off?" I asked.

Mike glared at me. "How many times we fish?" he said. "We never call one off yet!"

"OK, OK," I said. "Let's get at it. If we get lucky, the guy will get seasick and want to come back."

Mike grinned.

"Beer cold yet?" he asked.

"Christ," I said. "I just had Basil put it in the ice chest. How could it be cold yet?"

"I drink one warm, mon," he said. "Just for good luck."

The sea outside the cut was gray and rough, and the wind and rain were no help. I took some sandpaper to a couple of the No. 8 hooks Lucas was going to run back for marlin—without him knowing about it. Lucas was not known for worrying too much about the minor details.

Lucas ran a mullet on the port outrigger, a bonefish on the starboard rig and a balao on the flat line. The customer, whose name turned out to be Miller, took the fighting chair and I set his drags on the big Fin-Nors and the Penn reel on the flat line. Mike, as usual, ran a wooden teaser plug back behind the boat on quarter-inch nylon line. The big plug, used to catch the attention of billfish, sailed back about twelve feet behind the transom and at a depth of about four feet. It was festooned with red and green strips of rubber and weaved in the boat's wake.

When all the baits were out, Lucas climbed to the top of the ladder and stared astern. Mike and I retired to the bridge and Mike headed the big sportfisherman south with a following sea, hoping to cut down the sickening pitch and roll. By that time we were hanging onto both the wheel and tower struts in the towering seas. The customer maintained his seat in the fighting chair, but I noticed that occasionally he would reach into a side pocket of his jacket and take a sip from a bottle. I grinned and pointed it out to Mike—who had already noticed it, as he noticed everything on his boat.

We beat south for almost an hour from Bimini and nothing even surfaced to the baits.

Lucas changed them three times, switching the port outrigger bait to a rigged mackerel, just in case of a blue marlin.

Something did hit the flat line one time and cut the bait in half. Lucas and Mike saw the flash at the same time, but there was no hookup. Everyone agreed it probably was a barracuda, or maybe a wahoo.

It was about ten-forty-five and the weather was not getting any better, when Mike let out a yell.

"Billfish!" he shouted and pointed to the flat line in the wake. The customer was asleep in the chair and at the shout only stirred slightly. Lucas grabbed him by both shoulders and shook him awake. He immediately grabbed the nearest rod—which happened to be an outrigger rod—and jammed it into the fighting chair's gimbal.

I saw the bill and dorsal fin surface behind the balao in the wake, then disappear.

"Where the hell did he go?" I yelled at Mike.

"The teaser," Mike shouted and leaned over the edge of the bridge.

"Bring in the teaser, mon," he shouted at Lucas, who leaped aft and grabbed the nylon teaser line.

The billfish surfaced inside the balao and right behind the teaser plug. It whacked at it several times with its bill.

"Get the goddam thing in, Lucas!" Mike yelled. "He's trying to take the teaser!"

Lucas, fast on his feet, pulled frantically on the line. The teaser plug came sailing up to the transom, with the marlin right behind it, and then flipped into the cockpit.

"Good," Mike yelled. "Now maybe he'll drop back to the baits."

"The hell he will," I said. "He just hit the transom full speed."

"What?" Mike asked.

"You heard me, you big ape," I said. "Didn't you feel him hit that wooden stern?"

"You're crazy," Mike said.

Just then Lucas grabbed the big gaff and turned to shout at Mike.

"Captain!" he screamed. "He got stuck in the stern! The bill is into the wood!"

"Jesus!" Mike said.

Miller was still sitting in the fighting chair, posed for battle, his hands clasped around the butt of the rod. He was staring fixedly astern. The seas were monstrous and his face was ashen.

"Lucas!" Mike shouted down to the agile mate, who was poised over the stern, the big gaff raised over his head. "What the hell you goin' to do, mon?"

It was too late to ask. With a sweeping movement Lucas sank the big gaff into the tail section of the billfish and set his feet against the transom.

"Basil," he screamed, "get out here!" In a flash the big man appeared from the cabin and grabbed a length of line.

"No, no!" shouted Mike. "Dammit, that's a green fish! He'll kill us all!"

It was too late. Basil, his fine reflexes working without thought, flipped a loop around the tail of the billfish and the next thing we knew a blue marlin weighing about 250 pounds and fresh from the sea was in the cockpit.

Later, it was hard for me to remember exactly what happened. A young blue marlin, on 50-pound monofilament line and after an hour's battle, can still be a tough customer. In a cockpit — with no history of battle to tire it — the fish was a bomb.

Everything became a blur. I saw Lucas take one flail

from the massive tail and almost go over the starboard gunwale.

Basil threw his huge bulk on top of the thrashing fish, only to end up in a corner of the stern with blood running down one shoulder.

Through it all, Miller sat in the chair, his head swiveling as the battle raged around him.

Mike, letting the controls go, heaved himself off the bridge and landed within a few feet of the big fish. He grabbed a club and began pounding the fish on the head.

I leaped from the bridge, grabbed a small gaff and tried to snare the fish's mouth to get its head against something.

Everything melted into a melee of shouts, a pitching and yawing boat, a cockpit full of blood and great welts on our arms and backs from fighting the fish. Finally the throbs of the marlin grew weaker and I let go of the bill and saw Basil sitting astride the marlin, a triumphant grin on his face, holding a bloody club and slapping the wet body with glee. At that he fell over on his side on the bloody teak deck in complete exhaustion.

"Christ!" yelled Miller from the chair. "What a battle!"

"Oh shut up, mon," said Mike, nursing a tattered sleeve and lacerated wrist.

The wind had swung around to the north and we knew it was going to be a northeaster for sure. The seas built up and we beat it back past Cat and Gun Cay head-on into the gray cresting waves. By that time we had put away enough beer so that it was getting to be a funny story.

Getting across the bar at the mouth of Bimini harbor was a dilly with the tide at full low and the wind blowing the water out of the cut. The big Mead bounced once on the sand as we crossed. By this time Miller was just one of the boys — although I don't think any of us ever did learn his first name.

It was well after midnight and the rain and wind were lashing Alicetown like a small hurricane by the time we had retold the story for the fiftieth time and all turned in.

Mike got a letter from Miller two weeks later. Miller said he couldn't remember ever fighting a gamer fish.

Mike laughed so hard he almost choked on his early-morning can of St. Pauli Girl beer.

chapter nine

The Striped Marlin

By eight-forty-five in the morning we had already spotted seven marlin on the surface—12 miles off Puntita Santa Helena, Ecuador, on a heading of 240 degrees.

It was already hot on a March morning and the old wood boat had been chugging its way out of the harbor of Salinas since about seven a.m., its two diesels making not much more headway in the ground swells than a modest 5-8 knots. Captain José Gomez, the implacable skipper of the battered *Haridor*, nodded to one of his youthful mates and pointed to the outriggers. Both the boys sprang to and began to lower the outriggers as José opened the baitbox and laid out three rigged balao and a Spanish mackerel on the port gunwale.

I lowered the binoculars and pointed to a big wooden sailing canoe off the starboard side, bobbing in the swell as her crew of four fished over the side with handlines for bottom fish.

"Mostly they're after snappers and sea bass," I said to Constantine Kazanas, a friend from New York who had come down to catch his first billfish. He had just asked if the commercial sailing craft were out for marlin.

"Now and then they hook a marlin, though, and sometimes they land them on the handlines," I added.

"Jesus," Connie said. "I'll bet they need gloves!"

"From what I hear," said Gil Drake, my other companion, "they manage to snub the line around a peg or something and the main thing is not to get a hand or foot caught in one of the loops as the line whips out."

The mate had put out one balao on the port outrigger and the mackerel on the starboard one and had run them both back in the wake. I picked up one of the remaining baits they were about to run out on one of the two flat lines.

"They rig them a little differently here than they do up north," I said, showing the slim fish to Connie. "Notice they just sew the mouth shut with twine, then run the hook through the twine. It's almost a Catalina rig, but the mouth is held shut with the string and the hook isn't run through the upper and lower jaw. Off Florida and the Bahamas we sew the hook inside the bait and let it stick out the belly, but here there are so many fish they don't seem to care that much about the hook showing."

I handed the bait to one of the mates and reached for the suntan lotion. It was time to begin fishing, and the mates climbed atop the cabin roof to look for dorsal and tail fins of *el picú rayado* — the striped marlin of the Pacific, in my opinion the greatest jumper of the billfish family.

We had arrived by Braniff Airways late the night before on a flight from New York. The plane had stopped at Miami, where Gil, the Caribbean editor of *Field & Stream*, had joined us. After that it was Panama and Guayaquil and a two-hour car trip to the inn on the rocky point jutting out into the Pacific at the tiny fishing port of Salinas. With only four hours' sleep before the phone woke us at six a.m., we were not really quite awake yet in spite of coffee, breakfast and the sea air on the way out.

There were marlin fins and tails all around us just before we slowed to fish, but José assured us that there was no need to hurry, as there were many more on the world-famous fishing grounds near where the Humboldt current swung in close to the coast of Ecuador.

I had thought a few years earlier—after reading a few outdoor writers who had come down for several days' fishing and had written up the trip—that the current was just a few miles offshore and that one did not begin to fish until one reached it. This is not so. Most of the striped marlin and sailfish are fished for and caught only 12 or 15 miles off Salinas, and the Humboldt is approximately 70 miles offshore. With a speed of only about 5-8 knots cruising, the small fishing fleet here could not get that far out and back in a day to allow much time for fishing. There were a few larger sportfishermen about, but they were privately owned, and even they did not venture out that far often.

The black marlin, *picú negro*, is caught out near the main current. The blacks run larger than the stripes and sailfish, but most of the boats don't go after them. José told me that an occasional black is taken in closer during a few months of the year—September through December. There are *picù azul*, the Pacific blue marlin, to be caught here too, but they are far more scarce than the popular striped marlin. *Pez vela*, the beautiful Pacific sailfish—running far larger than its Atlantic cousins—is caught here frequently, and I had caught a couple of big ones several years earlier to the north of our present grounds. And occasionally one catches the great *espáda*— the broadbill swordfish.

"*Pesca!*" one of the mates shouted from above, and we all looked up to see the direction in which he was pointing.

There was a sickle-shaped tail visible in the gray seas about 100 yards off to the port side. José swung the boat to cut across its path while Gil, his cameras strapped around his neck, climbed carefully up to the top of the cabin.

"What do I do?" Connie asked.

"Nothing," I said. "Just stand here and see what the fish does. The marlin out here have so much food around that you never know when they are going to be interested in the baits. What the skipper will do is cut across in front of the fish and try to get it interested. Just stand here and wait. If it takes one of the four baits, we'll try and hook it. After that you get into the chair and we'll hand you whichever rod the fish is on."

"I still can't believe we're here!" he said.

I had met Connie a year earlier at a magazine seminar. He had just read a story I had written for *Field & Stream* on blue marlin fishing and said his life's ambition was to catch a marlin. I told him then that the next time I went to a good spot for billfish he was welcome to come along. I don't think he believed me. But a month before, when Gil and I decided to go to Salinas to try for some color action shots of jumping marlin, I remembered Constantine and called him.

The port outrigger bait swung within 20 feet of the cruising marlin, and suddenly I saw it thrash its tail and swing toward the bait, disappearing below the surface at the same time.

I stepped close to the port gunwale and put a hand on the Penn 50 reel in the holder. One mate took up a position beside another outrigger reel on the starboard side, and the other stood in the center of the stern where he could grab either one of the reels holding the two flat lines.

Fifteen feet astern churned a big wooden teaser plug, festooned with rubber strips. I saw a movement just behind my bait as Gil yelled, "Right rigger!" from the cabin roof.

I yanked the rod from the gunwale and looked at the port outrigger clip. It wasn't moving and I couldn't see anything behind the bait.

"Left rigger!" shouted Gil. "He's coming up slowly — watch it, watch it!"

The fish didn't take that one either and suddenly

switched to the flat lines, 20 feet closer to the transom.

"Flat line, flat line!" Gil yelled. He could see far better than we could from his vantage point. The fish switched to the flat lines, 20 feet closer to the transom. least two minutes before it simply submerged and didn't show again.

"What do you think?" Connie finally asked.

"You never know," I said. "Sometimes a marlin won't take a thing. Then about the time you think he's gone, up he comes and takes one of the baits."

But we finally had to accept that the fish was not hungry. We crisscrossed the area for ten minutes until we were convinced it was no use.

We spotted a number of other tails and dorsal fins in the next hour, but the marlin failed to rise to the baits. Then Gil shouted again from atop the cabin.

"Something under the left rigger!"

I didn't have time to figure what it was before the line popped from the outrigger clip and fell to the surface. The mate grabbed the rod as the reel shrieked and the line ripped off.

"*Dorado!*" yelled the other mate as the first boy advanced the drag lever and set the hook. The rod bent and I grabbed Connie and shoved him into the chair. The boy jammed the rod into his hands and I fitted the butt into the seat gimbal.

Connie's face was white with determination as he grasped the big rod and the boys and I began reeling in the other three lines.

A big bull dolphin cleared the surface 50 yards back and cartwheeled before it splashed back to the sea.

"EEEaaahhh!" yelled a mate, and Connie looked up at me, reeling frantically. "What is it?" he shouted.

"Dolphin," I shouted back. "A beauty. Keep reeling."

It was a good fight. Finally José shifted into low forward speed as Connie pumped the beautiful fish alongside. The boys finally gaffed it and Connie's face was a study as he saw the rainbow hues of the fish as it was held aloft. The fish weighed about 25 pounds.

"Beautiful, just beautiful!" was all he could say.

In the next hour we caught five more dolphin and pulled the baits in front of six marlin, none of which was interested. They appeared to be moving in a northerly direction for the most part.

I was opening a bottle of Club beer, the native brew bottled in Guayaquil, when Gil's voice rang out from above.

"Fin back of the right outrigger!"

I had gotten used to it enough to finish taking the cap off the bottle before coming up the companionway to the deck. There was nothing on the surface behind the skipping balao.

"Still see him?" I asked.

"No, no," Gil said, "I don't think so. Wait a minute . . ." His voice trailed off.

I took a swallow of the cold beer and placed the bottle in a holder. I just reached the port gunwale when the line snapped from the rigger and I saw the geyser of water where the port bait had been. I grabbed the reel and thumbed it for a second until I felt the weight and a slight tugging. Flipping the lever to more drag, I struck quickly two times and raised the rod tip. I knew instantly this was no dolphin; both my arms jerked out straight.

"Marleen!" yelled one of the mates as the fish came up not 30 yards out, climbing slowly into the hot air, twisting, writhing and thrashing its silver-and-purple-striped length in anger at the bite of the hook.

"My God!" Connie shouted. "Look at that! *Look* at that!"

It was a young, "green" striped marlin that had no intention of being caught. The first jump was a good 10 feet into the air, and it was followed by a dozen more.

After that the fish made a series of greyhounding leaps. It must have made twenty of them before it sounded, leaving Connie in a state of near collapse from shouting and pointing.

Even after another ten minutes the fish made some spectacular leaps close to the transom before being gaffed—giving Gil some great action photos and splashing water over us all.

It took us another five dolphin and two more hours to get Connie his first marlin strike. It was a blind strike—the fish never appeared on the surface. The mate grabbed the rod; the 50-pound mono on the reel was rapidly being peeled off. Connie fully expected the fish to be another dolphin as the mate set the hook for him and handed him the rod. He felt the power of that fish as he leaned back in the chair and hung onto the arched rod.

The fish didn't jump. It had missed the bait on the strike and the hook had been set deep into the shoulder as it turned away. However, it was a good-sized marlin and it was headed away from the boat at full speed.

"Jesus!" Connie said as the reel whined.

I stood behind him and turned the chair so that he was facing the fast-disappearing line.

"Just hang on," I said. "Let him tire himself out."

"Why doesn't he jump?" Connie asked

"Some of them don't," I said. "This guy is one of those tough ones—maybe figuring to fight it out below!"

I was reasonably sure it was a marlin. The chances of it being a tuna were slim. I turned and looked at José, steering the boat carefully. I pointed at my forehead, then at the side of my neck. He nodded slowly, agreeing that the fish was probably foul-hooked. It wouldn't matter, however, as long as Connie got it in.

That was one of the toughest battles I have ever seen for a fish that size. Connie fought an exhausting, sweating and panting battle. The several buckets of cold salt water I poured over him helped.

The fish finally gaffed after about twenty-five minutes, and we saw where the hook was. Connie was so happy he couldn't have cared less.

A half-hour later with the sea almost at dead calm, I hooked a big marlin that put on a magnificent show of jumping. The first series of jumps never seemed to stop. I was fighting the fish standing up with a leather belt, and even after the third series of jumps I couldn't believe it.

There was a boat about 100 yards from us, and on

about the fourth series of frantic leaps the fish started by going straight up until both Gil and I estimated its tail must have cleared the surface by at least the fish's own eight-foot length. We could hear the people on the other boat as the fish came down and headed toward them. With a dozen more jumps it went behind them, taking at least 500 yards of the 50-pound braided line I had on the reel. It was a magnificent fish.

Gil wanted some subsurface shots of the striped marlin. When I finally managed to get it close to the boat, Gil swam around it with his underwater 35mm camera. He was wearing a snorkle, mask, and flippers. The mates watched him swim, occasionally scanning the horizon for a fin. *"Tiburón"* (shark) one of them said as he held a gaff. I knew the fish was hooked in the corner of the mouth, so there was little chance that any blood would attract sharks.

We boated the fish and hauled Gil aboard. The temperature was then close to 100 degrees and there was almost no breeze. The heat in the cockpit was stifling, and we stayed in the shade of the roof. I think Connie had given up on his chances of catching another marlin by the time José glanced at his watch and looked at the big butte guarding the entrance of the harbor to the east.

"Una mas," he said quietly, and I looked at my watch. It was two-thirty and we would have to stop trolling at three-thirty in order to get in by five p.m. — the usual end of a fishing day. I nodded and shrugged.

The big marlin hit not more than two minutes later with no warning at all. None of us saw the fin or tail. One of the mates almost fell from the cabin roof to the cockpit deck in his haste to strike the fish. Connie was in the chair and fast to a 160-pound striped marlin before he knew what was happening.

That fish did everything in the book. The marlin jumped, jumped, jumped and continued to jump — at distances up to 600 yards from the boat — until not only the mates but Gil, José and I were hoarse from shouting.

Not only did it jump far out but, even within gaffing distance, it burst from the sea to wallow behind the stern, thrashing in rage. It pounded against the boat even as it was being gaffed and almost tore one of the flying gaff lines from the hands of one of the mates. When it came aboard—glowing with lavender color and sheer silver in the afternoon sunlight—nothing in the world could have spoiled the day for Constantine.

chapter ten

The Barracuda

Most big-game fishermen consider the barracuda a damned nuisance. I do at times—especially when the quarry is tuna or billfish and barracuda cut off trolled or live baits on the kite lines.

Regardless of the size, there is never much trouble subduing a barracuda on big rods. These predator fish strike savagely, and many an angler has thought he had either a big wahoo, king or yellowfin tuna on for the first few moments. But a barracuda, at least in deep water and on heavy tackle, does not put up much of a battle after a few initial bursts of speed. It is for this reason that it has never gained much of a reputation as a game fish. After I found out about its game-fish qualities I was delighted to read that Zane Grey and his brother used to fish for them with light tackle at Long Key before World War I and considered them one of the best sport fish around. Van Campen Heilner also caught them on light tackle and thought them terrific fighters.

I knew nothing of this, however, until I had a chance to fish for them on the bonefish flats of Cat Cay with light spinning gear. My three sons were living in Ft. Lauderdale, and I had the small boat over at the island during the Christmas holidays. Johnnie and Donald came over, for a week each, and we caught lots of fish. Both boys enjoyed barracuda fishing best. I am sorry I couldn't take Jimmie over, as he has always been the most enthusiastic fisherman of the three, but he was only about eight then.

We used light spinning rods and eight-pound mono-filament line. We fastened wooden silver and cobalt-blue plugs to the lines with a light eight-inch cable leader to keep the barracuda's teeth from cutting the lines. The six-inch-long plugs were equipped with two sets of treble hooks, and when trolled across the flats would dive to a depth of about a foot and stay there. The water depth would vary from a foot to several feet, depending upon where the various channels were from the lighthouse on the rock jetty to the southern end of South Cat Cay. Fortunately there is little in the way of coral rock on the east side of the two islands, or I would have had to replace props fairly often. As it was the blades were well chewed by conch shells as the prop churned up a wake of white marl every so often.

I would watch for the big predator fish through po-larized glasses as one of the boys stood between the two light rods stuck in the console seat rod holders. Barracu-da usually travel either in pods of four to six or in pairs, but sometimes a lone fish would sight the wriggling plugs from at least 50 feet away. The fish would streak about halfway to the boat and then stop to get a better look. That's when I would shout for the boy to get ready, and usually just about then the incredibly fast fish would be almost upon the lure. At that depth the strike was an explosion of spray and coral sand as the huge jaws clamped down on the plug and its sharp hooks. Anyone who has caught these great fish only on big rods in deep water would be astonished at the fight they put up. The bigger fish are up to five feet long and weigh 30 to 40 pounds on the average. Many will leap into the air on feeling the bite of the hooks and soar 20 feet or more on the first few jumps. We had some smaller ones jump as many as fifteen times in a row—jumps that would make a flyrod-hooked Atlantic salmon look slow in comparison.

The boys and I were not trying for records, just fun. It took fishing pliers and a tight grip behind the head with a heavy glove to release these big, toothy battlers. We released most of them—only to catch the same fish sometimes a few days later. They never grew smart enough to resist those wriggling plugs. A good fish would take twenty-five minutes to whip, and even after getting them close to the boat, they would make sudden last-minute runs that tore line off the small reels. We kept a few each day because Curly, the bartender at Cat Cay, loved to eat them. He tossed them into the freezer room and later sawed the frozen lengths into steaks. He had no concern about the occasional instance of ciguatera, the poisoning possible from eating large, old fish (presumably because the barracuda had eaten smaller fish that actually carry the toxin themselves, such as the puffers and others). He admitted he had heard of people getting sick from eating them and even losing all their hair, but he said he liked eating them too much to worry about it.

I hooked a heavy barracuda in the channel between Cat and Gun Cay one day as I was going out for marlin. I was using a red-and-white-striped saltwater spoon about eight inches long on one of the light boat rods and 9/0 reel filled with 12-pound mono. The spoon had one double hook on the aft end. That barracuda was well over six feet long, jumped only twice—falling back with a tremendous splash each time—and got away when I stupidly let it get behind the coral reef jutting out from the dump on the north tip of Cat, and the line parted. I have always wondered how much that rascal would have weighed. Nelson Bryant, who was with me at the time, hazarded a couple of guesses, but I suspect it was to make me feel worse at losing the fish.

It was while fishing for barracuda at Cat—on a windy day—that I saw A. J. McClane pull off one of the fishing stunts that have made him a light-tackle legend. The wind had been blowing from the northwest for twenty-four hours and we were unable to go out into the Stream on the west side of the island, where we had planned to try for big fish. Bing McClellan and A. J.'s wife, Patti, were along and we were on my Boston Whaler. Since the flats were in the lee and the water calm for several miles south, we decided to try for big barracuda with light rods and level-winding plug-casting reels. We had gotten to about the channel between North and South Cat when I eased the controls into neutral and we drifted in about two feet of water. A. J. rigged up a yellow wooden torpedo-shaped plug about six inches long. It was a floater, equipped with two sets of treble hooks. As A. J. flipped it out about 50 feet from the boat I looked at him.

"What you after with that?" I asked.

"Oh, anything," A. J. said in his maddening casual manner. "Lot of fish will take a plug on the flats—tarpon, jacks, barracuda, bonefish."

No fisherman is ever too old to learn something new. I forgot that for a moment. I should have known better. The trouble was I had been stalking bonefish on the flats for years and knew how spooky they could be.

"Bonefish?" I said, looking at Bing, who sensibly shrugged. "On that thing?"

A. J. didn't bother to answer, but twitched the big plug a couple of times and the lure disappeared in a boil of water. The casting reel shrieked as a fish headed southeast.

"That bonefish should go about eight pounds," said A. J. as he handed the arched rod to Patti, who calmly held it over her head. After ten minutes she brought the fish alongside, and Bing netted it. It weighed just a fraction more than eight pounds.

"Lots of times," A. J. said, "bonefish, either alone or cruising the flats with another big fish, will hit a plug. They take bait fish when hungry." He unsnapped the plug and tossed it to me. "Try it."

I tried it for a couple of hours and caught five barracuda on it, but never a bonefish. Nor have I yet, but I do have that plug hanging on the wall of my den—to keep me from forgetting again that an angler never gets smart enough to know it all.

One of the biggest and most spectacular barracuda I ever saw caught was one by Pat Smith when he and I were bonefishing on the tiny flat near Walker Cay in the Bahamas. The wind was too high that day to let us go after marlin and sailfish with Les Flato aboard the *Sea Lion*, but we had both taken billfish the day before—me a nice blue marlin and Pat a good sailfish.

We had hoped to make it a grand slam that next morning by taking a white marlin, but the wind turned and blew out of the northeast, ruining all the blue-water plans. Rather than spend the day in the bar or at the swimming pool, Pat and I found a guide and pounded across the stretch of open water to the small bonefish flat a few miles away. The tide was wrong and we caught no bonefish, although we saw several small schools. As we were about to leave in the afternoon and return to the marina, Pat found a pod of about six big barracuda lying in about 10 feet of water in a channel. Several casts to them with spinning rods and small spoons drew only a half-hearted follow from several of the medium-sized ones. There was one huge fish in the school. Standing on the bow of the bonefish skiff, I could make it out lying close to the bottom in light blue-green water. Pat was fascinated by the size of that fish. He wouldn't leave until he tried everything in his tackle box. I finally got tired of watching him cast to the unresponsive monster and walked back down the bank toward the skiff to get a cold beer from the ice chest.

"I think I'll try bait," I heard Pat say as I walked on the white sand. I stopped and looked at him. "What kind?" I asked.

"Oh . . ." He looked in a plastic sandwich bag he had tied to his belt. It contained some shrimp and pieces of conch the guide had chopped up for him to use for bonefish. "I think I'll try conch on him." I shook my head as he fastened a big piece of the rubbery conch on the bonefish hook. He had ten-pound mono on the medium-weight spinning reel. I walked toward the boat, idly thinking about getting a camera and taking some scenic color shots while Pat ran out of ideas to catch the big barracuda.

I never saw that fish take the bait. Later Pat said he cast the glob of conch ahead of the 'cuda, let it sink slowly until it reached about the right depth, then moved it in a series of short jerks. He said the big fish simply turned, rose slightly and swallowed it. He was so surprised he didn't set the hook until the fish settled back to the bottom. When he did set it, I heard a whoop of excitement and saw the guide, ahead of me, point back to where Pat stood. I turned just in time to see that fish at the top of a jump that must have been 25 feet straight up! Because of the small pool it didn't go far horizontally, but it hurled itself into the air and climbed for altitude. When it came down it sounded as though a 12-foot skiff had been thrown into the water.

I made a run for the camera, but the fish was too big to make more than about two jumps. By the time I got back to Pat the long, loglike fish was thrashing in the center of the pool. When that didn't get rid of the hook it made two streaking turns of the 30-foot-long pool, yanking the rod almost out of Pat's hand. Half an hour later Pat had the fish in the shallows, and it still fought him as he walked it down toward the boat where the guide had a long-handled net. That guide, however, was having none of a barracuda in the shallow water! Pat finally had to slide it up on its side, where I socked it with a big gaff and finally got some pictures. I don't recall if we weighed that fish when we got it back to the dock, but it was more than five feet long and heavy-bodied. We both agreed if I had gotten an action shot of that first jump it would have been some picture.

My biggest barracuda was never weighed either, but it was close to six feet long and was caught at Treasure Cay on Abaco. We were making a bonefish movie with A. J. as the angler and had tried for two days to get some good flyrod sequences, but the weather had been against us. It remained overcast, making it hard to spot fish, and thundershowers kept passing over us every hour or so. The barometric pressure was low and the fish were not feeding too well. A. J. was fishing from a bonefish skiff with an old friend, guide Joe Sawyer, acting as his pole man. Two camera boats glided along near him as he stood in the bow looking for bonefish schools. I had given up on the bonefish and was on a larger 24-foot boat anchored in the mouth of a small channel on the east end of a small island. The current had our boat facing upstream on an outgoing tide and the water, gurgling at about six knots, poured past us and fanned out on an expanse of flat to the east. I was tired of doing nothing, so I picked up a glass rod belonging to Bud Brownell, who was sunning himself on a forward deck. I dug in the skipper's battered tackle box until I found an old wooden floating plug with rusty treble hooks. From one sailfish wire, I made a leader about a foot long and fastened a big swivel on the end, and after sharpening the hooks with a piece of torn sandpaper, I stood up on the transom and flipped the plug out on the flat. I let it run out several hundred feet with the current before flipping the bail closed and twitching the plug. As the floating plug reached the end of the arch, I twitched it again. There was a sudden bulge just beyond the plug and a flash of silver, but it was too far away to see what had made the commotion.

I cast at that same area for half an hour until I began to think there was nothing there. I decided to make a few more casts and to let the plug float farther out on the flat.

By that time the plug was in about a foot of water and there was not a thing in sight on the expanse of white bottom.

I will never know where that big 'cuda came from, but it erupted from beneath the plug and took off across the flat in a series of jumps that could be heard up on the foredeck where Bud was. I heard the pounding of feet as he came over the top of the cabin and dropped to the deck behind me.

"What the hell was that?" he asked, shading his eyes to see where my line was stretching. "It sounded like a marlin out there!"

It jumped like a marlin too. It took almost an hour to land that fish—what with the current aiding it and only about 150 yards of 10-pound mono on the reel. It was a huge barracuda and it took both A. J. and me to get it. I transferred to the skiff and, with the help of Joe, poled out to fight it.

There are all sorts of stories of barracuda attacking swimmers and wading anglers. I have never seen a documented case, although Bahamian friends swear they know it has happened. I have been down close to them in scuba gear and have had them follow me slowly while snorkeling for lobsters. They are somewhat unnerving—remaining still in the water and watching when one looks at them. If you swim toward them they will back up slowly—much like a pickerel or a big northern pike will move in reverse—but I have never seen them attack. I know their unbelievable speed and am never really at ease when I am in the water.

One of the most eerie stories of barracuda was told to me by Captain Henry Phillips, a longtime skipper who worked for Hatteras at Highpoint, N.C., and spent many years with the boats in the Bahamas. He was en route one day from Florida to one of the cays—West End, I think—and it was a calm summer morning with the sea glassy and a hot sun shining. He was running a big Hatteras sportfisherman alone. He began to feel hungry and decided to stop for lunch. He shut off his engines and slowed the boat to a stop in about 15 feet of clear water over a white sandy bottom. Henry told me he wanted to stretch and get off the bridge for a change of scenery. He got a sandwich from the galley and walked back to the cockpit, where he sat on the gunwale next to the transom and unwrapped the sandwich. He was about to take a bite when he glanced into the water. On the bottom, like so many logs, were hundreds of huge barracuda. They just lay there, baleful eyes looking up in the clear water. He estimated some at seven feet and longer.

Henry said he knew the sportfisherman was 45 feet long with a fiberglass hull. He said he sat there for another moment, looking at the sky and the sleek boat and feeling the hot sun beating down on his bare arms. There was no sound on the big expanse of calm Gulf Stream surface. He told me he slowly rose to his feet, climbed to the bridge, started the big marine engines and headed for the islands . . . feeling relieved only when he was doing about 20 knots on a calm sea.

chapter eleven

A Boat Is for Fishing

Back in 1969 when Willard F. "Al" Rockwell and other members of an investor group bought internationally famous Cat Cay in the Bahamas from Jane Wasey, daughter of the late great host and fisherman "Uncle Lou" Wasey, I had a chance to spend a lot of time there. The island is situated about 50 miles east of Miami and 15 miles south of the great fishing island of Bimini.

Cat Cay was practically shut down from the standpoint of docks, electricity, water, fuel or repair facilities. The once-posh mansions were unoccupied hulks cracked from the lush Bahamian jungle growth, the docks were rotting wooden pilings, and the once-manicured island roads and bicycle paths were choked with undergrowth. The only feature of the island not changed since the halcyon days was the fishing. It was probably even better that year than it had been in the forties and fifties because of less fishing pressure. Before 1965, when Hurricane Betsy had smashed into the island—ripping out the docks, smashing yachts and sportfishermen against the curving rock jetty and leaving some stranded high on the island near the administration building—dozens of boats a day had fished at the famous dropoff just out from the channel running between North Cat Cay and Gun Cay.

Across the famous flats that ran from the rocks southwest of South Cat Cay almost up to Bimini came the schools of bluefin tuna each year about the end of May and first of June. They poured across these flats by the thousands on their northward migration, and many a great name in the big-game fishing world—Tommy Gifford, Bill Carpenter, Annie Kunkle, Ernest Hemingway—had known the thrill of battling the big bluefins there.

But it was not just the tuna that made this dropoff famous. The water changes from the aquamarine blue of the 60-70-foot-deep flats to the royal blue of the great Gulf Stream depths not more than a quarter-mile west of the cut. And it is there that the big blue marlin, white marlin, sailfish, dolphin, wahoo, kings and sharks roam the edge of a sheer underwater cliff that drops more than a thousand feet to the ocean floor.

I had fished for years in big boats along the dropoff from north of Paradise Point on North Bimini down as far south as Riding Rock Light, below Sandy Cay—trolling the Stream in all types of weather and at all times of year. I had taken blue and white marlin from the big fiberglass Hatteras sportfisherman Rockwell kept on North Bimini in the 1960s. Also I had fished in the sturdy wooden boats out of Bimini—crewed by great native fishermen like Mike Hinzey on his *Striper II*, Ray Pritchard, and a half-dozen other fine boatmen who know that stretch of water—taking billfish as well as the streaking wahoo and my favorite food fish, the dolphin. In the days before the Bimini Big Game Club folded up and Mickey McCann left for the mainland, my idea of going to heaven was to bring in a couple of small dolphin and have them broiled at the club and served with just lemon juice and a little garlic sauce. It is still my version of the promised land—although when Sylvano Carmalini was the chef at Cat Cay in early 1970 he did some things with freshly caught and broiled Spanish mackerel that were almost beyond belief.

I had fished for years in the big boats—the Bertrams, the old Owens out of Bimini, Jack Tar's fine old Pacemaker at West End, Les Flato's beautiful *Sea Lion* out of Walker Cay, the Chris Crafts and Ryboviches out of Palm Beach, Miami and Ft. Lauderdale, Allen Self's trim Perma-Craft at North Key Largo, the Huckins and Mead sportfishermen used by the Crown Colony Club at Chub Cay, and Al's beautiful Hatterases, *The Laurie* and *Hatterascal* at Bimini and later at Cat Cay. But somehow I wanted to try small boats. I just got to thinking one day about Tommy Gifford and his legendary *Stormy Petrel*, which he had fished out of Cat Cay before and after World War II and upon which so many great big-game fishermen and women had tangled with big fish. It was a small boat by the standards of those days and certainly would be considered so today. Yet he, like me, had been fond of kite fishing and had wanted a boat which was not only seaworthy, but fast in emergencies.

During the 1968 Boat Show in New York, while prowling among the 21-to-38-foot sportfishermen and getting more discouraged by the day, I came across my answer.

A gent whose name I do not know but to whom I shall ever be indebted had designed a weird-looking cutty-cabin version of a Boston Whaler—16 feet 9 inches long, with a double-layered fiberglass hull filled with liquid styrofoam which dried to give ultimate flotation. It had a comfortable, cushioned skipper's seat mounted amidships just aft of where the cutty cabin—molded into the hull—flared up into a windshield with vertically swinging glass panels that could be opened on hot days. She was as ugly a small boat as I have ever seen, but I saw something in her that apparently no other big-game angler there did. She had two bunks with storage space under each, a head, a small folding galley table and storage room inside the waterproof cabin for lots of tackle, food and emergency rations, and she could be sealed off warm and dry against cold or driving rain. I suspect Dick Fisher, president of the company that makes the famous Boston Whaler open fishing boats, hoped to market this as a "family" boat. I was thinking of the perfect shallow-draft, tough, fast, maneuverable, warm and dry, trailerable boat that could be used as easily for tarpon in the Keys, bonefish on the flats of Bimini or trolling for marlin off Cat Cay. Fisher had named the model the "Menemsha" after the historic whaling port on Martha's Vineyard. She had a big bait box molded into the hull and storage space to burn under the center console seat. She could be powered by any outboard motor big enough to make her hull plane, and she had a fiberglass seat facing backward against the console. I could install a gimbal and use the seat as a fighting chair. On a conventional sportfisherman, the chair should be able to turn, but this small boat was as maneuverable as a sports car and carried Morse controls mounted atop the cabin, so it could be turned to keep the angler facing the fish. The cutty cabin also opened in the bow by an ingenious system of "clamshell" doors, which allowed a fresh breeze to blow through on hot days and provided room for a fisherman to stand and cast from the bow. She shed water over the bow like an ocean liner.

She was trailerable and small enough to handle in traffic on a busy highway. Unsinkable and seaworthy as any boat her size in the world (and many a lot bigger), she cruised at 30 knots with an 85-horse Johnson outboard—her unique hull skimming across the tops of a light chop or planing almost without vibration on a calm sea. My two oldest sons and I fitted her with 15-foot telescoping glass outriggers and four strong gunwale rod holders, and installed big bitts for a flying gaff rope and heavy cleats for lashing big fish to her. We gave up the idea of a gin pole, relying on her speed and stability to lash fish alongside and run them in to a harbor.

I may own other boats besides the Menemsha, but it is doubtful if I shall ever be as fond of one as I was, and still am, of that ugly fishing machine. We pounded her through every test we could think of in the cold and gray seas off New Jersey—from the vicious swells off Sandy Hook to the treacherous rips off Cape May Point. We took albacore, school tuna, big blues and stripers with her in bad weather and good, and dolphin, sails, white marlin, kings and amberjack off Ft. Lauderdale. Trailered into the Florida Keys, she kept us dry in tropical line squalls that sent bigger open boats scurrying to the home marinas. She glided across a few inches of water in the Keys, where we took bonefish and permit, and with the motor tilted up, she could be poled close to the schooling tarpon we took with spinning and fly tackle.

But her real test came when, on a whim, I decided to run her over to Cat Cay and try for the big fish.

There were a number of people who told me I was mad, and I have no argument for that—what big-game fisherman is not? It was just one of those things that comes to possess a fisherman who loves the sea and big fish, and the more I thought about it the more appealing the idea seemed. My oldest son, John, who, I fear, inherits some idiotic tendencies from me, considered the idea a real challenge. And so it was one spring afternoon that we set out from Ft. Lauderdale on the 70-mile run to Cat Cay, loaded down with plenty of big-game tackle, rations for weeks, emergency equipment and enough tools to rebuild the Menemsha in midstream.

Only one thing marred the trip: an unexpected and unforecast west wind sprang up. Anyone who has ever sailed the Gulf Stream knows there is no way to get an accurate forecast of weather. We had been able to run about three-quarters open the first hour, paralleling the shore until we could just see the tips of Miami Beach hotels and then taking a new heading direct for the island. The Stream flows north and remains relatively calm when a breeze blows from the southeast, but it reacts violently to a northwest, north or northeast wind. By our third hour out we were not only taking heavy seas on the port bow but were forced to run at less than half speed in order to keep the bow high and the stern low.

Fortunately we had a number of 6-gallon tanks aboard, in addition to the two main 12-gallon tanks in place under the console. Nevertheless it was a pounding, brutal trip in six- and eight-foot seas, and we sighted the light at Sandy Cay at dusk. It was beating northward directly into the teeth of the seas after that until we hit the lee of the tip of South Cat Cay and were able to anchor and secure some gear that had worked loose. With the motor off and the cabin zipped up we could heat some tea on a canned-heat stove on the small galley table, wash down some canned meat and crackers and listen to the transistor radio while we warmed up a little from the soaking we had taken.

Rather than ride out the night at harbor, we went on our last auxiliary tank and made the run along the western lee shore of South Cat Cay and cut around the point on North Cat where stood the old Kitten Key Bar and water tank. We were unable to cut between North and South Cat Cay because of low tide and were forced to run head-on into seas up the west side of Cat to the cut between the north tip and Gun Cay—where we slid through the narrow channel and had to take massive following seas all the way from there to the old lighthouse perched on the end of the jetty at the mouth of the harbor. When we eased through the old dock pilings and tied up next to the concrete seawall, the longtime dockmaster, Jimmie, came out of the customs shack with a flashlight and stood looking down at us as I handed John the big-game reels to wash off under a freshwater faucet before they started to corrode.

"I talked to you this morning on the radio phone," Jimmie said incredulously. "You cross in this wind?"

I nodded.

"You must be a churchgoing mon," he said, "to come across in that little boat!"

I climbed onto the dock and made sure of the lines

before starting toward the administration building, Jimmie waddling along beside me.

"I'm not so much a churchgoing man, Jimmie," I said. "But I am a lucky one. The good Lord didn't give me too many brains, even for a fisherman. But he gave me a boat I could take around Cape Horn without drowning . . . little as she is."

And in the next eight months the Menemsha fished out of Cat Cay. At first nobody paid much attention to her, but as the months went by, and my fishing partners and I began bringing blue marlin, whites, mako, wahoo and yellowfin tuna into Bimini and Cat Cay—many taken on kites—the talk began to spread about the ugly little fishing boat and the crazy American who went after the big fish with a boat short enough to be a dinghy on many of the yachts and sportfishermen that put into Bimini and Cat.

Many a fisherman, forced to idle away a couple of days aboard his big boat while the west wind churned up the Stream, asked to go out with me when I took the Menemsha out in the lee of Gun Cay and Cat and trolled the flats for huge barracuda. The big, ugly and savage predators prowled the flats—unfished for in years—in pods like wolf packs. Many were five and six feet long and when hooked in shallow water—sometimes not a foot deep—would put on an aerial display of jumping that would put an Atlantic salmon to shame. Many a day we pulled into the docks with four or five huge, toothed 'cuda in the bait box, their tails hanging out one end of the four-foot-long well. During Christmas vacation of 1969, Johnnie, who was then fourteen, hooked, fought and landed a 38-pound barracuda on eight-pound spinning tackle not 100 yards from the jetty east of the docks. My Don, then twelve, caught one nearly that big one spring weekend near South Cat Cay. Even Al Rockwell, who usually preferred his 45-foot Hatteras, *The Laurie*, for big-game fishing to the west of the island, finally succumbed after hearing some tales of the sport and made it a regular practice to whip these tigers of the flats on light tackle when he got a few hours free and could clamber aboard the Menemsha.

The hands at Brown's Dock and the other marinas at Bimini became used to the stubby little boat putting in to weigh some fish every few days.

And, oh, the fish we lost and never saw! Those are the ones that remain in my memory. Doug Gifford, a young civil engineer who was charged with rebuilding the island, would go out with me whenever he could find time. A former Lafayette linebacker, Doug was an immensely strong gent, and I have seen him—arms straightened and back bowed in the cockpit of the whaler—battling a huge fish that never jumped or neared the surface after taking trolled baits. And even after the 80-pound braided line had parted, we never knew what the fish had been. They were not tuna—the season being wrong—but could have been big sharks. The billfish we knew, but there were huge amberjacks near the reefs, and one time I played a giant grouper for two hours before losing it after it had taken a trolled feathered jig in the cut as we were headed out for wahoo.

We rode out a tropical line squall one day in the lee of the concrete wrecked ship after getting caught on the flats between Cat and South Bimini—riding at anchor, drinking St. Pauli Girl beer and playing gin rummy, snug and dry as the seas pounded the far side of the historic hulk and the winds shrieked overhead.

I caught almost every big-game fish of the area from the Menemsha except bluefin tuna, which only pass the island for about a two-month period each spring. I am confident I would have taken one of them if I had not decided to bring the boat back from the islands in the spring of 1970 and trailer it north again. I ran her across the Stream, alone at the helm, one beautiful day in April, and made the trip in two and a half hours.

The radio was playing music from a Miami station, I rode the console seat, a cold beer in one hand and all the great world of sky and wondrous royal-blue Gulf Stream around me.

I brought her skimming into the slot at Ft. Lauderdale, her hull planing smoothly across the wakes of hundreds of other boats and a Cat Cay pennant streaming from one outrigger. I am sure that people seeing her from the windows of the high-rise hotels and condominiums, if they thought about her at all, thought she was just another speedboat—and not the great fish-fighting lady she is.

The Menemsha is shipshape and berthed in the fine fishing port of Cape May, New Jersey. Donald, who loves her as I do, acquired her as a high school graduation present. He keeps her a gleaming white and all gear spotless and ready for fishing.

And, knowing Don for the skipper he is, I would not be too surprised if she shows up one of these days at the new concrete docks of Cat Cay or alongside the pilings of a rejuvenated Big Game Fishing Club at Bimini—or prowling the dropoff west of Gun Cay, her motor muttering as she runs in slow forward, baits skipping the waves behind her in search of big-game fish.

chapter twelve
The Mako

*I*t was a clear, breezy morning in May and I had run the little boat across the flats from Cat to Bimini in time to meet A. J. McClane, coming in on the Chalk Airline flight from Miami at nine a.m.

While waiting for the yellow-and-black amphibian to land in the harbor I had looked up two local youngsters who were my secret weapons when it came to locating live bait. I had sent word over the day before on the Chalk flight to the kids, whom I had met through their uncle, Mike Hinzey, when he was a corporal on the Bimini police force. They could come up with any bait wanted if given an hour's notice. The boys kept a wire-screen bait cage suspended under Brown's Dock. They were real friends of mine, not only because I paid them well for fresh live bait, but because we were fellow fishing pals. I went out with them several times in their battered wooden skiff and anchored in the channel just off Alice-town, where we would handline bonefish for trolling baits.

It always amused me to run into bonefishermen in the local bars who regaled the audience with the stories of the several four-to-six pound bones they had managed to catch with spinning gear after a full day on the flats. The bonefish is a great sport fish in shallow water, no question about it. I have spent many a happy day stalk-ing both them and permit on the flats with a fly rod— and hope to spend many more. But what a lot of bone-fishermen don't know (and probably don't care to know) is that anyone can catch bonefish in deep water on conch, sandcrab or shrimp—especially when they school up under dock pilings or lie in the harbor chan-nels.

I once won a pretty sizable bet from a gent in the Big Game Club who thought I was out of my mind when I mentioned that not only could I provide him with a doz-en bonefish bait for marlin within two hours but I could get every one of them the same size.

My two little chums came up with the dozen in an hour and twenty minutes—all handlined from beneath the docks. They had to throw back several dozen more to get them all the same size. They could have done it fast-er, but they had to wait a bit for a better tide.

This morning they were both lying face down on the hot gray planks of the dock, watching schools of bar jacks and mullet swirl around the pilings below them. Small barracuda were suspended in the blue-green water next to the barnacle-encrusted posts, waiting for a pil-chard or snapper to stray too far from its own school. The water was a veritable aquarium of trigger fish and snap-pers of all sorts weaving in and out among the shadows and sunlight.

The boys had several dozen grunts, as many assort-ed snappers and hundreds of pilchard in the bait cage. Since they were not after bonefish this morning, they didn't even bother to use bait. They had tiny gold hooks—about a size 18 or 20 salmon-egg hook—tied on four-pound monofilament, which they lowered into the schools. When the hook reached the school of pilchard, they would spin the line between thumb and forefinger and the tiny gold hook would give off flashes of sunlight. A fish would take it within a second and the boys would casually flip it up, catch it, and toss it over into their bait tank.

I patted Arthur on the bottom and he grinned when he saw who it was. Phillip rolled on his side and smiled.

"We got plenty, mon," he said. "All you need."

"Great," I said. "The tub is in the boat. I'll be by in half an hour. Got to meet Mr. McClane on the plane. He has the air pumps."

The boys went back to work as I headed for the airline ramp. The plane was just banking over the pink-colored hotel on South Bimini and would make a landing right down the channel in the harbor, heading into the southeast wind of about 10 miles per hour.

A few minutes later the clumsy Grumman Mallard waddled up the concrete ramp and the pilot swung it around to face the water again before cutting the engines.

A. J. was about the fifth passenger off. He was carrying his favorite reel in a bowling-ball case and a small cardboard box. When he cleared customs, we walked toward the docks; A. J. carrying his suitcase for a week's stay of fishing. I carried the cardboard box.

"I picked up two electric pumps from Fishermen's Paradise in Miami," he said. "They don't cost that much, and what the hell, if one goes out you always have the spare. They don't last that long anyway."

I nodded and we walked down the dock to where the Menemsha was tied up. Several local fishermen were peering into the cutty cabin, which had the clamshell doors open for cool air. I asked them how the fishing had been as A. J. stowed his gear. It was just small talk—expected in the Bahamas of all fishermen. I knew how the fishing had been in the area for weeks. A number of good blue marlin had been brought in and plenty of whites. Wahoo were running well, too, plus dolphin all along the Stream when one could find a floating weed-line or some debris under which they could hide.

I started the 85-horse outboard. It made a burbling sound of exhaust vents as I backed the boat out of the slip. I swung it around the corner of the dock and headed for the slip where the kids had the live bait. As they scooped the small fish into a large plastic garbage can, I took one of the small electric pumps from the box and stowed the other under the console seat. Pulling the battery box out from under the stern seat, I took off the cover and fastened the leads of the motor to the terminals. The little motor instantly started humming and I dropped the plastic tubes into the bucket. Twin streams of air bubbles came up from the bottom instantly.

"Good," grunted A. J., as he took off his shirt and reached for some suntan lotion. "That should keep them healthy all day."

I paid off my two cohorts, who immediately headed up the dock toward the store across the street where the lady sold candy, ice cream, soft drinks and souvenirs.

A. J. tossed his slacks into the cabin and changed to a pair of swimming trunks as I swung the bow toward the mouth of the harbor and added speed until the hull planed and the vibration ceased.

I had both my favorite boat rods in the gunwale holders. One was rigged with the 9/0 Penn reel carrying 600 yards of 50-pound braided Dacron. The bigger rod held an old but well-maintained Ocean City Model 612 on which I had carefully wound 900 yards of new Cortland Micron line in the IGFA 80-pound class. It was a newly developed line of much smaller diameter than the Dacron or mono and had almost no stretch factor. The wet-test strength was 72 pounds.

A. J. slid his favorite rod from the cabin. It was his own and I kept it on the island most of the time for when he could come over to fish. He dug his reel out of the case and fastened it to the reel seat as the boat hit the first waves coming in over the sand bar. The seas were running about two to three feet and it looked like a perfect day for fishing. A. J. had 800 yards of 30-pound line on the reel, and as I swung the bow slightly toward the southwest he began measuring off 15 feet of double line and started tying his Bimini twist. I cut the power back and kept the bow up to reduce the pounding from the small seas. Tying a twist and an offshore swivel knot is not easy in a dock, much less in a small moving boat, but A. J. is one of the fastest and best knot-tiers I have ever met. I had rigged up a batch of 15-foot piano-wire leaders on #7 and #8 hooks and had them carefully coiled inside the console bin.

By the time A. J. had his terminal tackle rigged we were over the dropoff and into the royal-blue water about a mile and a half southwest of Bimini. I ran the boat for another five minutes, then slowly pulled back on the Morse control and allowed the bow to settle into the slight chop. I slipped the throttle into neutral and we drifted north on the Stream as I took out the big wooden kite line spool and jammed it into a starboard gunwale holder.

"Which kite we using?" A. J. asked as he finished slipping the wire leader loop into the snap swivel.

"I think the medium," I said, sliding the orange silk kite from where the three kites were held by snaps on the cabin roof. "The wind seems to be holding steady. We can always switch to the light one if she dies down any."

The colorful kite caught the breeze almost at once and climbed up about 50 feet above us before I snubbed the line down on the spool and dug a couple brads out of a side pocket. I ran the 80-pound through it, then slipped it into the clothespin snap at the 50-foot mark. I reached into the tank and managed to corner an eight-inch-long grunt. I slid the point of the #8 hook through the back just forward of the dorsal fin and not deep enough to injure the spine, so the fish could swim freely. Then I flipped the big Ocean City reel onto free spool as I ran the kite out to the 100-foot mark. My bait wriggled high up in the air as I put a six-inch pilchard on A. J.'s line and then ran both lines out until the kite flew high above us and almost 200 feet to the north. I fed the line through my fingers until the live bait on my line finally reached the water, where I let it swim just below the surface. A. J. did the same until the two baits were swimming in the blue water about 50 feet apart. Occasionally the rise and fall of the kite would pull one or both of the small fish a foot or so into the air. They would wriggle frantically until either the kite lowered them back or I brought them down with a few turns of the kite spool.

A. J. stretched his arms above his head and yawned. I caught another grunt, slipped a #7 hook through it and lowered it into the depths behind the transom on a wire leader weighted with a six-ounce sinker. I fed out several hundred feet of line until the bait swam far below us, then set a drag of about 30 pounds on the 9/0 reel and stuck it in an aft holder, for whatever gamefish might strike from the depths.

The hot sun burned down pleasantly as we rode the Stream, surrounded by the blue sky and darker blue water, with the white glare of the boat cut somewhat by polarized glasses.

"We're in business," A. J. grinned as he slung a leg over the gunwale and shaded his eyes to watch the baits.

I watched a big Chris Craft yacht churn out of the west and pass us by several hundred yards heading for the mouth of the Bimini cut. Several people on the fantail waved to us and we waved back.

The contented feeling of fishing began to come over me and I leaned on the seat back—savoring the gentle roll of the small boat and the warmth of the sun on my shoulders.

The shriek of the reel jolted me upright on the seat and I instinctively reached for the big rod close to my right hand. A. J. had grabbed his rod from the gunwale and was staring at the spot where the two baits were when I realized the stern rod was bent double in the holder. I swung from the seat and grabbed the rod. The butt slapped into the leather Bimini belt socket and I felt the weight of a diving fish.

"Damn," I breathed as my arms were jerked downward, "this one means business."

A. J. had no reason to reel in the other lines, since in kite fishing only the baits are in the water. He sat on the gunwale and watched me as I slid into the fixed chair and fitted the rod end into the gimbal.

The fish continued to bore downward, and I increased the drag until the rod tip arched almost to the level of the surface. Finally the fish stopped, but did not come up. It tried to dive several more times, causing the reel to whine each time. Slowly I began to gain line by pumping, but it was hard work.

"Yellowfin tuna," A. J. asked, "or a shark?"

"Don't think so," I said. "It's not making any kind of a run, like the yellowfin should. And it's not circling any. Feels like a big grouper, but if it is, it's one hell of a grouper!"

"Have fun," A. J. grinned.

Fun I had for about twenty minutes. By the time I got the fish up close to the surface I knew I had been in a battle. It turned out to be a big amberjack—one of the strongest fish I know for its size. We estimated its weight at 50 pounds. A. J. snipped the wire leader at the hook and released the fish to swim slowly away in the clear depths.

There had been no action at the surface baits, so we brought them in and put fresh fish on them before settling down to play the waiting game again.

Half an hour later, a kingfish came slashing in from the open sea side and took one of the surface baits without slowing down. The first we knew of it was when I caught the flash out of the corner of one eye and A. J.'s rod was snapped into a bend as the streaking fish hit the taut line and preset drag.

It was a good battle and we gaffed and finally slid the king over the side and into the fish box. It later weighed out at 30 pounds and provided a fine evening meal, broiled and served with melted butter and garlic sauce.

For lunch, some time after we had drifted past Paradise Point on the west shore of North Bimini and were well on the way toward Great Isaac's Cay, we ate ham and cheese sandwiches and dug some cold St. Pauli Girl beer from the ice chest. The German beer—the popular brand in the Bahamas for years—tasted fine in the hot sun.

I took a fairly small bull dolphin half an hour later on the big rod—which was no contest—but we kept the 12-pound fish for food.

At about one-thirty a dorsal fin suddenly appeared behind the nearest surface bait and A. J. grabbed the rod and waited for the fish to strike. It circled the bait and started off. I reached over and started the motor, which I had turned off some time before to conserve fuel. I wanted to be able to swing the boat when the fish made its first run.

The kite rose on a sudden puff of wind and raised the bait from the water. I reached for the kite spool to lower it back into the water, but it wasn't necessary. The disappearance of the bait must have sparked the interest of the billfish, for it swung back and intercepted the bait just as it touched the surface again. There was an explosion of white water as the marlin slashed at the live bait, and the 30-pound line slapped to the surface from the kite-line clip.

"Line down!" I yelled as A. J. pointed his rod tip at the spot for a moment, then set the hook with several short jerks to the upright position.

"Whoooeee!" I shouted as a small white marlin came 10 feet out of the water and tail-walked 30 feet across the surface before starting a series of jumps toward the line of green Australian pines that was the distant shore of Bimini.

I slipped the throttle into forward and swung the stern toward the jumping fish as A. J. chose to stand up and fight the white with the belt socket. I reached over and turned the kite-reel spool a few turns to get my outside bait fish out of the water, just in case the fish changed direction.

The white was a very game fish and put up an aerial display that made the entire day worthwhile. It took A. J. about fifteen minutes to subdue it on the 30-pound line. We passed a plastic tag through the dorsal fin of the fish, then released it. We guessed the weight at about 70 pounds.

That called for a couple of cold beers and a discussion of the fantastic fighting qualities of the white marlin. The wind held and we put two new live baits on and continued the drift, moving north at approximately six miles an hour on the current. Private planes flew over us now and then, and an occasional jet bound either to or from Freeport and Florida passed high to the north of us.

I was idly contemplating the swimming baits and A. J. had climbed on top of the cabin to sun himself, knowing I could reach all three rods if anything hit, when there was a flash under the outermost bait. I rose and stepped into the cockpit, where I could easily reach the big rod.

I was beginning to think I had imagined the flash, when the surface at the outbait erupted in a geyser of white and the line snapped from the kite-line pin.

"A. J.!" I shouted as the fish—whatever it was—hit the end of the slack line with the strike drag at about 25 pounds.

The big rod was almost yanked from my hands as the fish took out line on a run. I set the hook hard, twice, as A. J. came off the top of the cutty cabin and flipped on the ignition key. He cranked his bait at least 10 feet into the air and spun the wheel to get me facing the direction of the fish. Then he reeled in the deep line.

"What you think?" he yelled as the line tore off the reel.

"Keerist!" I said, hanging onto the bucking rod and trying to back into the seat where I could get a solid rest and a gimbal. "I don't know what it is."

At that moment, the fish took to the air in a spectacular series of jumps. Not only did the big fish jump high—at least 15 feet on each jump—but it did end-over-end somersaults, throwing itself with complete abandon into the air and smashing back to the surface, only to reappear in a matter of seconds with another series of leaps.

"Mako!" A. J. yelled. "One hell of a mako. Ease up a little on that drag. That fish is going to jump for a while, and the drag is increasing each time it takes more line out. Jesus, I'm glad you have that 80-pound on!"

This was my first encounter with a mako. I had caught sharks before—whites and hammerheads off Montauk and Cape May some years before. They had put up a stubborn battle but had stayed below the surface. I had never seen a jumper like this one before.

I think that series of jumps must have totaled at least a dozen. A. J. later agreed, but at the moment we were too busy to count. After the jumps, the shark stayed below the surface but continued to take line at will. I didn't worry too much because of the 900 yards of Micron.

The fish went into a frenzy a few minutes later out at about 700 yards and jumped another four or five times. I finally began to notice a slowing down of the reel spool at about 800 yards.

"How big do you think he is?" I grunted, trying to get a little line back, but realizing the reel spool was still turning steadily.

"It's hard to tell when a fish is moving as fast as that one is," A. J. said, "but I would think between three and four hundred pounds at least. I know one thing. He's not going to be any cinch to bring aboard this boat."

"I have news for you, chum," I muttered as I tried to gain line. "What makes you think I want that fish aboard?"

The shark suddenly decided to swap directions and the line went slack. I thought I had lost him.

"Reel, reel," A. J. said. "He's headed back. I'll try and get a belly in that line." As I frantically reeled, he eased the boat into forward and swung in a circle to the west. It was a few moments before I felt any weight on the line, but finally I noticed the increase in tension. A. J. slowed the boat slightly as the line became taut again. The shark apparently had headed directly back to where it had been hooked, but now it had some additional drag from the billow in the long line. I was grateful for the small-diameter line now. The longer the line, the greater the pressure and the risk of breaking, but the risk was less with the reduced friction of the Micron.

For the next hour I worked that fish as I have seldom worked either billfish or tuna. It would tear up the surface when it felt like it, making any number of jumps, as high as the first series. When it decided to sound, it did so—causing me to pump until my arms, legs and back grew numb. When it headed for the boat, A. J. circled it to give me tension again. We repeated this time after time. I think if I had had a line of less strength, I would have lost the mako on the first series of jumps and runs.

Two hours later, I had the big fish circling the boat—not so much like a whipped fish as like a wolf circling a moose foundered in the snow. I had the feeling it was waiting for us to give up, rather than the other way around.

"What do you want to do with this character?" A. J. asked.

He needn't have asked. He knows me well enough. This was my first mako and I was determined to win the battle. When I didn't answer he shook his head.

"OK," he said. "We'll try and take him, but it's going to be a bitch. This is no billfish. We have a good flying gaff, and that's a help. As long as we make sure it's fastened to the big stern cleat, I don't think he can jerk it away. If we get him alongside, I'll take the leader and you sink the gaff."

I looked at the wake the mako was making as it circled us about 30 feet out. I wasn't too sure about that stern cleat holding—although it had held for some big blue marlin.

"One thing I think you should do," A. J. said slowly, "is to fight him the rest of the way with the belt. I've got to turn off the motor and raise it to the up position. If he starts going under the boat at the last minute, we're going to lose him on the props or lower unit."

I nodded, standing up and fitting the big rod end into the belt socket. "If he starts circling too much and you can't keep the rod up, start walking him around the boat," A. J. said, getting out the flying gaff and nylon line. "One thing with a mako," he went on as he spread out a tail rope on the stern seat, "is they jump at the last minute. Believe me, pal, you don't want this guy in the boat with us—not with those teeth. When you put that flying gaff into him, get it into the back *behind* the dorsal fin. That way you can maybe get his tail up a little. With a jumper like him you don't want to gaff him forward. He may go straight up—taking you and the gaff with him." I nodded, trying not to think of the mako in the cockpit with the two of us.

When A. J. had all the gear he wanted ready he looked up and nodded.

"OK," he said grimly. "Tighten that drag down a little and horse him in. He may fight awhile more, but I think he's had it."

I pushed the drag up some and leaned back, pumping the big rod. The mako thrashed on the surface at first, but finally began to give line, easing toward the boat. When within 10 feet or so of the hull, the fish suddenly dove under the boat. I reacted by instinct, plunging the big rod straight down and hanging on. It was a good thing A. J. had raised the outboard motor because it would have been in the way. As it was, the fish came back around the stern and surfaced on its side, close to me. It had its mouth half open and presented the wickedest set of irregularly spaced teeth it has been my luck to see in many a year. I suddenly began thinking about the sportsmanship of tagging and releasing game fish.

A. J. slipped on a pair of cloth gloves he yanked from the waist of his swimming trunks and reached for the leader, just as the mako exploded from the surface and arched at least 10 feet into the air. For one awful moment I thought it was coming down in the boat. But it came down slightly off the starboard stern and only its tail whacked the corner of the gunwale as it entered the water, showering us with spray.

We both ducked and I was yanked to the side like a wet dishrag as the shark dove, pulling the rod tip down with it.

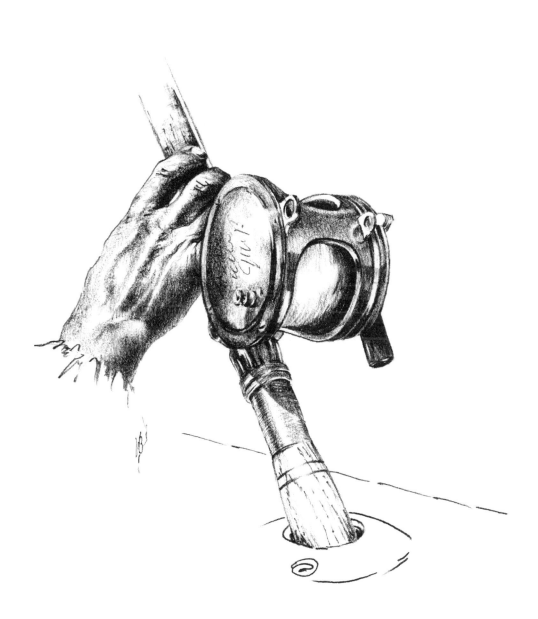

By the time I had straightened up and got control again, I had a feeling we both had some reservations about taking this fish. But we did share one trait—we were beginning to get annoyed at the mako. It was now becoming a contest.

"All right," A. J. said, "you ugly bastard. That did it. When he comes up again I'm going to take that wire quick. Jam that rod in the holder and zap him with the gaff. If he starts to jump, let go of the line. Trust the cleat to hold. If it doesn't we won't have to worry about him for a while."

The mako came to the surface this time and I had a feeling it was for the last time. It was spent, but its malevolent eye kept watching us as we moved into position.

A. J. reached out, took the wire leader and drew the fish close to the hull. I dropped the rod into the holder—not before releasing the drag just in case it dove and we were involved with some leader coils—and picked up the big flying gaff handle. Remembering what A. J. had said, I reached out and pulled back hard against the back of the shark several feet behind the dorsal. As the hook sank home, I unscrewed the handle and slung it back into the cockpit, diving for the tail rope at the same time.

I felt water showering over me as the mako thrashed against the side of the boat. A. J. was bracing his foot against the gunwale, holding the wire in both gloved hands. Peering over the side, I could see the fish was having trouble getting its tail into the water, thanks to the gaff being far enough back in the body.

I leaned over the side and tried to pass the rope under the narrow part of the tail to snap the line swivel and received a clout on the right arm that almost paralyzed me. I staggered back and held onto the transom.

"Get the motor down!" A. J. yelled. "And get some power to it. Drag the son of a bitch backward for a while until he learns some manners. I'll let go of the wire when we get some headway. I think the gaff will hold."

I may have set a world's record in lowering an outboard and getting it started. The half-inch nylon line of the flying gaff was less than 30 feet (by IGFA rules). When the boat was underway, the big shark began to swing away from the hull. A. J. let go of the wire leader and allowed the mako to slide astern, where it was towed backward, held by the big gaff hook. The moving water continued to pour into the gill slits of the shark as we circled slowly—the boat cockpit a shambles of rope, seawater, line and wire leader. The live-bait bucket was on its side and the deck was covered with wriggling bait fish. I leaned against the console seat and started to laugh. A. J. looked at me and then at the big mako being towed astern, still struggling convulsively. Then he slid to a sitting position against the side of the cockpit, in a pool of water and wriggling fish, and began to laugh, too. "Tow the bastard for an hour," he gasped. "I want to be sure he is all the way dead before we get him near us again!"

I towed him for about twenty minutes, while A. J. and I drank a few beers. Then we eased the motor into neutral and brought the shark alongside. We tail roped it and lashed it against the hull firmly with three lines.

The weight made the boat list to starboard, but we shifted most of the gear on board to the port side to compensate. With the motor in full forward we were not able to make the hull plane, but it did make some progress with the bow high—perhaps 5-8 knots.

It still took more than an hour to make the cut at Bimini. We went into the harbor under full power with the sun low on the horizon and had the mako hauled up on the scale at Brown's Dock. It weighed 356 pounds—no record on 80-pound line and the big rod, but not a bad mako, especially for my first. We ate the kingfish that night and told some good stories about that shark. We got to bed late and somewhat unsteadily, I must admit.

The next morning a lady about to board the Chalk flight to Miami came down to the dock and saw the mako lashed to the scale. Wanting to get a picture of herself by the big fish, she stood beside it and handed her camera to a local skipper. As the skipper was taking the picture, the mako feebly opened its jaws and closed them with a resounding click. The lady damn near fell off the dock.

chapter thirteen
The Tarpon

*I*t was June and it was hot and the humidity was high — ideal bonefish and permit weather for the Florida Keys.

Permit are fine fish and I had never caught any on a fly rod. I had caught two the year before at Chub Cay in the Berry Islands, but both had been on a spinning outfit, with sand crabs for bait. There is nothing unsporting about this method of fishing. It is an effective method, and a permit is more than likely to get away from you no matter what tackle you use. I just wanted to take one on a flyrod, and the Keys were the best place to try.

Oscar Godbout and I had been over in the Everglades for a couple of days trying to catch some big largemouth bass from an airboat out of Frog City on Alligator Alley, but the fishing had been slow. We had taken a couple of fair fish, but the big ones were sulking in the grass and no popping bug or weedless plug could bring them out. Oscar had gotten a couple of good columns out of it for the New York *Times*, and Sid Latham had been puttering around us in another airboat taking some color shots. We had gotten back to Miami and Sid was due back in New York for some meeting or other.

Since we had done a couple of stories on sailfish and kings off North Key Largo with Allen Self, we had pretty much all the big-game stuff we needed. Breakfast was almost finished and Sid was about to leave.

"Well," said Oscar, after putting away his usual three-course breakfast, "it's either we go to the pool and look at the stewardesses, or we fish."

We had been staying at the Miami Springs Villa, the home of a stewardess training school, and the scenery at the pool at all hours of the day had been pleasant.

"I worry about you two," Sid said, getting up and shaking hands. "It's been lots of fun. I think we may have some good stuff—both the largemouth and the sails." I shook hands with him as Oscar pushed his chair away from the table and stood up.

"So long, hotshot," he said.

"Good luck with the permit," Sid said, "although I don't envy you the heat."

We watched him thread his way between the tables before we paid the cashier and walked to Oscar's battered station wagon in the parking lot. The back was loaded with rod cases, tackle boxes, suitcases, camera gear and assorted junk Oscar always threw in. We had checked out before breakfast and had the several hours' drive to Islamorada ahead of us. We had originally intended to drive down to Key West, but only had the day to fish and couldn't spare the time. Besides, guide Jack Brothers, a displaced New Yorker who had given up Fun City years before for the beauty and peace of the bonefish flats, had assured us there were plenty of permit about. Oscar had caught one the year before in lower Biscayne Bay, but this was his first trip to Islamorada.

The holes in the boat rack atop the station wagon set up a maddening moaning sound as we sped south of Homestead on U.S. 1.

"Why the hell don't you put tape over those holes?" I asked. "Or throw the rack in the back?"

"Oh, I don't know," Oscar said casually. "I kind of like the sound. And if I take the rack off I'll just have to put it back when I put the aluminum canoe on."

"It sounds like your transmission's falling out," I said.

"It could be," he said lazily. "With the expense account the good gray *Times* gives me I'm lucky to be driving instead of walking."

It was hotter than the proverbial hinges when we pulled up at George Hummel and Bill Pate's tackle shop to call the guide.

Jack's wife answered the phone and told Oscar that Jack had gone to Miami to pick up a new outboard motor. She said he would be back that evening.

"Damn!" said Oscar after hanging up. "That blasted Irishman forgot all about us coming down."

"When did you call him?" George asked. "That doesn't sound like Brothers."

"Call him?" Oscar asked. "Hell, I told him a couple of months ago I'd be here the first week in June. You can't depend on anything any more!"

"Christ," I said and looked at George.

"Any other guides around this time of the day?" I asked. It was almost ten o'clock.

"Nope. I was over at Bud and Mary's for breakfast when most of them went out. Everybody had a charter."

"What about boats?" Oscar asked.

"There's a couple at the dock for hire," George said.

"Fine," Oscar said. "Jack here knows the water. We can just tool out for a couple of hours and try for some fish. If it gets too hot or the fish aren't hitting, we can always come back and sit in a cool bar."

There was a 13-foot Crestliner with a 9½-horse Evinrude and an 18-foot Mako with a big 85-horse Johnson for rent. We decided on the big boat because of the heat.

Running speed cools one off in the hot weather. We got sandwiches made up, put some beer and ice in the chest, stowed the rod cases and tackle boxes, and finally set off down the narrow channel toward the flats. The high tide was expected at two o'clock, so there wasn't much water over a few of the bars as we headed for the flats to the west of the highway bridge, hoping to find some areas of turtle grass and shallow water where we might catch either bonefish or permit feeding on the incoming tide.

Oscar had his big rod rigged by the time I slowed the boat near a couple of small mangrove islands and tilted the big motor up. There was absolutely no breeze and we floated on the glassy water as though in a large, muggy fishbowl. I could feel the sweat begin to pop between my shoulder blades as I slid the 9-foot flyrod from the aluminum case and started fitting it together. I took the big reel from a leather case and fitted it to the reel seat. I had rigged up a 15-foot leader to the 30 feet of shooting-head floating flyline before leaving the hotel. The tippet at the end tapered down to 3X—perhaps a little light, with a breaking test of about 5½ pounds, for big permit, but they are a spooky fish and have good eyesight. There was about 150 yards of 12-pound linen backing on the reel. After stringing the #10 shooting head through the guides, I tied on a light-green keel fly Bing McClellan had tied up and swore was the best bonefish and permit fly around.

Oscar had on a yellow keel fly some guy had given him in Miami and was perched on the bow platform scanning the still flats. I picked up the wooden pole and eased the tip into the white sand. The silence was unbroken except for the slight crunching sound of the pole each time it touched the sand, and the gurgling of water passing beneath the transom. Off to our right a great blue heron took off with a hoarse croak and winged across the water to a less disturbed mangrove clump.

The heat was suffocating and the glare of the burnished sun on the water made me squint even through polarized glasses.

"Mud," Oscar finally said, pointing off to our right. I

could see the milky puffs in the water where a school of fish had fed recently on bottom worms or crustaceans.

"Hard to tell whether it was bones or permit," I said.

"More than likely bonefish," Oscar said slowly, "the water as shallow as it is. Let's try a little more to the left toward that deeper channel. Maybe we can spot a school coming in on the tide."

I nodded and shoved the pole into the sand.

We saw nothing but an occasional barracuda and a collection of snappers for the next twenty minutes until suddenly Oscar pointed to our left, where the white sandy bottom shelved off into the blue channel.

"School of bones coming," he said, crouching a bit. "Swing the bow left a little. If they keep coming along the edge I may be able to reach them."

I swung the bow left, then shaded my eyes to look. I finally saw a school of perhaps thirty fish headed almost directly toward us. They were in about a foot of water and appeared to be cruising slowly rather than feeding. Oscar stripped line out at his feet and began false-casting as the school approached. I felt the old excitement as I watched the lead fish come closer.

Oscar dropped the fly well ahead of the school and let it sink slowly to the bottom.

"Good, good," I whispered. "They should pass right over it."

Just about the time the lead fish reached the spot Oscar picked up the rod tip slightly and twitched the yellow fly. I could see it move slightly on the bottom. Strangely enough, three or four fish passed over it without making any move to pick it up. I thought they were not in a feeding mood, but suddenly one of the fish swung from the school, tilted nose down and picked up the fly.

"Ugh," Oscar grunted as he set the hook, the rod held high over his head. The big rod bowed sharply and the reel sang as the fish took off across the flat to our right.

"Yeehooo!" Oscar laughed. "Look at him go!"

It was a good fish and it made four or five long runs. Oscar was a fine fly fisherman, having learned as a kid in his native Vermont. It didn't take him long to bring the fish alongside. I netted it and we held it up for a picture. It weighed eight pounds on the pocket scale. We slid it back into the water and released it. The silvery fish swam off slowly at first, then suddenly took off on a straight run for the channel.

"Here," Oscar said, reeling in his line and stepping down from the forward casting platform. "Let me pole for a while. Let's see you top that bony."

He opened the ice chest and took out a beer. "Want one?" he asked.

"Nope," I said, stepping up to the bow. "It's a little early yet. Let's see if we can find another school and then I'll join you."

We poled across that flat for another half an hour without seeing any bonefish or permit. There was a basin off to our right where the bottom was covered with turtle grass. The tide had been feeding in through the channels for some time now and the water was getting considerably deeper. It was getting harder to stay in the shallows. I looked out to the right and noticed a disturbance on the surface of the water in the center of the basin about 100 yards away.

"Oscar," I said, shading my eyes with a hand, "what do you make of that?" I pointed. Oscar, can in hand, stood on the seat and looked.

"Holy cow!" he said softly. "Tarpon!"

I felt my heart speed up. "You're kidding," I said.

"The hell I am," he said. "I'll tell you what that is. Tarpon move in a circle like that in spawning season. They keep right on going around and around like that for hours. I caught the biggest tarpon of my life in one of those daisy chains at Big Pine Key a couple of years ago. Sit down and hand me that rod. I'll reel in that line while you get the other spool out."

I nodded and handed him the rod. I dug the other spool out of my fishing vest. We had been fishing for sailfish a few days before with the other spools and I had

200 yards of 20-pound linen backing on the reel and 70 feet of #11 weight-forward floating flyline. The leader went down from a 3-foot section of 60-pound mono, where it was fastened to the flyline with a nail knot smoothed over with airplane glue so it would slide through the guides easily. After that came another 3-foot section of 30-pound mono tied to the bigger length with a blood knot. Another blood knot took it down a 12-pound section, then to a 12-inch length of 80-pound mono shock leader. Oscar was threading this through my guides as I fitted the big reel to the seat. My hands were trembling as I did it. I had caught several tarpon from New River at Ft. Lauderdale and the St. Lucie Canal near Stuart, Florida, but none had been over 12 or 15 pounds.

Oscar snapped open his fly box and took out a red Keys Tarpon Streamer fly on a #4 hook and quickly fastened it to the end of the shock leader with a regular clinch knot. He reached into his tackle box and grabbed a pair of fishing pliers and tightened the knot as hard as he could.

"OK, chum," he said, handing me the rod. "Now if we get lucky you are going to have the time of your life. I'll get you as close to those monsters as I can, but remember they can see a long way in this clear water and they may spook. Lay that fly slightly ahead of the one you pick, but don't let the leader come across its back. Fish him just like you would a trout. But the main thing," he said as he picked up the pole and began pushing the boat slowly toward the disturbance on the surface, "is to make damn sure all the line you strip out is coiled at your feet where you don't step on it. Keep the other coils in your left hand, and if one of those beasts takes the fly, right after you set the hook don't look at him. Keep your eye on the coils as they go out, because they are going to be going fast! When the coils are all gone, then you raise that tip as high as you can, look up if you still got him on, then hang on and play him with the brake. OK?"

"OK," I said over the pounding of my heart. I could see the huge shapes now as they circled slowly in about six feet of water. "My God, Oscar," I said. "They look like submarines! How big do you think they are?"

Oscar stopped poling and looked for a moment.

"Hard to really tell from here," he said softly, "but a couple of those big ones could go well over 100 pounds."

My mouth was dry and I licked my lips as we inched up to the circling fish on the still surface.

"OK," Oscar said quietly. "Strip off all the line you need to make a cast of at least 60 feet and maybe more. Start your false-casting as soon as we get into range. Pick the one you want. Try to pick one that is sort of away from the others, not one that's swimming with his nose close to the tail of another. It can see the fly better."

I nodded and started stripping off line. When I had enough out I started the casting. Only the swishing sound of the line broke the silence. The fish were moving as in a strange ritual dance. I saw one slightly off to my side of the circle swimming slowly, its dorsal whip out of water and the tip of its huge tail breaking the surface lazily. A couple of hauls and I shot the line at a spot about 6 feet in front of the fish. The line began hitting the surface about 30 feet out and the leader followed and slapped to the surface—I thought like a telephone pole hitting the water, but perhaps it was just my imagination. The fly settled to the surface about 10 feet too short.

"Not quite," Oscar breathed. "Try it again. At least they didn't spook. Don't set the hook too hard if he takes it. I honed that hook as sharp as a needle. It will go in with luck. They have plates all over them. The only thing to worry about is busting that 12-pound tippet."

I had the line back and started the casting all over again. I knew it had to be close to 80 feet to where the big fish swam. I picked another fish on my side of the circle. I tried to time it so that the fly would hit quite a bit ahead of the big head, but I misjudged it by a few feet and the streamer fly landed about three feet ahead of the fish and a foot or so to my side of it.

"Oooohhh," I heard Oscar breathe.

The big fish simply tilted its head up, opened its jaws the size of a peach basket, closed them on the fly and sank beneath the surface. I struck with a snap of my wrist and remembered to look down at the coils. I heard the sound of water being churned up as if by a waterspout, but I didn't look until the last of the coils had left my hand and the platform at my feet. When I raised the tip and looked up the tarpon was suspended against the horizon 150 feet away on what must have been his third or fourth jump. The fish was twisting viciously in the air at least 10 feet above the surface. The sound of Oscar's wild yell mingled with the dry rattling sound of the big fish's gill plates and the crash of water.

My arm was nearly yanked from the socket when that fish hit the end of the billow in the line. I have seldom—with perhaps the exception of the bluefin—felt such unleashed power! Another and another jump across the surface of that lagoon until I couldn't believe the fish could keep it up! I had 100 yards of backing out and the fish showed no signs of slowing down when Oscar dropped the motor down, pushed the starter button on the console and started after the fish.

The jumps became slower but the fish was still moving away from us at a terrific speed. I felt the boat pick up speed as Oscar added power.

"Reel, reel," he shouted over the motor noise. "He's not about to stop for a while!"

The fish had stopped jumping now but was swimming steadily toward the middle of the distant bay. I could see the many-spanned highway bridge, hazy in the distance to the east. The other side of that was the Atlantic.

"He's headed for the Bahamas!" I shouted above the noise, and Oscar laughed with glee.

"How you like big tarpon?" he shouted.

"My God!" was all I could say.

I gained some line in the next thirty minutes while we simply kept up with the swimming fish. It was indeed heading for the bridge—swimming against a strong bay current and a still-incoming tide. I applied the brake as much as I could and finally felt the fish tiring. It had been almost an hour and both my arms and back were numb from the strain when the fish suddenly decided that fighting the tide, current and the big rod was tiring him too much. A mile or so short of the bridge it suddenly made a circle in front of the boat and Oscar slipped the throttle into neutral. The boat coasted to a stop in the still water as the fish took to the air in another series of dazzling jumps.

"I think you got him whipped," he shouted. "I'm going to raise the motor in case he starts going under the boat."

I was too busy with the fish to watch him. The fish made several more twisting, frenzied leaps, falling back to the surface with a loud crash each time. Finally it simply began to come in on its side, its huge gills flaring each time it took a breath.

Oscar reached for his camera as the fish came alongside. I heard him take several shots as the big tarpon lay on the surface not more than a few feet from the boat.

My rod was bent double and I looked at Oscar.

"What do we do with this thing?" I laughed a little unsteadily at the thought of gaffing it.

"Hell," Oscar said. "We can gaff it and haul it aboard if you want, but I don't know what you'd do with it unless you want it mounted. They aren't any good for eating."

I looked at the great silver length of it and shook my head. "No," I said, "I don't see any sense in having it mounted. It's a hell of a fish, though. How big you think it will go?"

"Oh, close to 100 pounds," Oscar said matter-of-factly. "I doubt if it will go quite that, maybe 90."

I looked at it again. "Well," I said, lowering the rod tip a little and letting the fish's head settle in the water, "cut him off. Let him grow to weigh 150 pounds and I'll catch him again."

"No need to cut him off," Oscar said. He reached out, took the fly in his thumb and forefinger and removed it from the fish's mouth. The big silver king simply sank slowly out of sight in the milky water of the bay. I sat down.

140

"Congratulations, pal," Oscar said, shaking my hand. "You have just been kissed by a tarpon."

I looked at my hands. They were shaking from nerves and strain.

"Now," I said. "*That* is something else!"

"You bet your fanny it is," Oscar said, lowering the motor and punching the starter button. "And I have had all the excitement I want in this heat. Let's get back to Bud and Mary's and get into an air-conditioned room. One big tarpon is enough for any man in his life."

I don't know about that, I thought to myself as the boat began to pick up speed across the flat surface of the bay. I don't know about that.

Appendixes

Appendix A
Equipment and Technique

THE BIG-GAME FISHING BOAT

A boat for big-game fishing should meet certain requirements. It should be seaworthy enough to stand fairly high seas. It must have enough power to get to the fishing grounds—regardless of how far out. It must be able to cruise while trolling all day, and return to port or a mother ship at night. It should be maneuverable enough to speed up smartly and to make tight turns. Preferably it should allow the skipper some altitude to spot fish ahead of the boat, feeding sea birds, and game fish coming up from below the baits.

A sportfisherman should be equipped with a fighting chair if possible, although many big-game fish are fought with a rod belt. Fighting chairs come in all shapes and sizes, from the folding lightweight chairs used on small boats to the intricate and sophisticated equipment on the big sportfishing boats. Ideally the chair should contain a gimbal or socket in which to place the butt end of the big-game rod. The best chairs provide a footrest so that the angler can use the strength of his legs in battling a fish, armrests, an adjustable backrest, and provisions for a fighting harness. The best are also capable of swiveling in a 360-degree turn upon a pedestal mounted solidly on the cockpit deck.

The adequately equipped sportfisherman should also carry two outriggers. The smaller boats often mount collapsible fiberglass or aluminum outriggers, which extend out about 15 to 25 feet, and the larger boats generally mount more sophisticated outriggers of aluminum, capable of extending out 45 feet. Obviously the farther out the baits can be trolled on either side of the wake of the boat, the better the chances are for attracting the attention of cruising gamefish.

The boat should have at least four solidly mounted rod holders—preferably two in each gunwale at the sides of the cockpit—in order to run two outrigger lines and two flat lines. The two flat lines are positioned at different distances behind the boat, in the wake, but closer to the boat than the outrigger baits.

A fish box is necessary. The larger boats usually can accommodate one across the inside of the transom or below deck in the cockpit area. The smaller boats may have to improvise, but many small sportfishermen today have the fish box built into the hull.

The tuna tower of the large sportfisherman provides a place for the captain to run the boat high above the deck level. Small sportfishermen do not provide as high a platform, although lightweight towers may be installed. Many smaller boats have a center console steering system, which enables the angler to get considerably higher above the surface of the water.

A transom door which swings open close to water-level is ideal for sliding large fish into the cockpit. Many of the large sportfishermen are equipped with these. On the smaller boats the anglers must rely upon hauling the catch over the transom or gunwale after it has been brought to the boat and subdued.

A gin pole with a system of pulleys may be mounted on both small and large boats. It provides the best method of raising large fish above the water surface. Many gin poles today are made of lightweight aluminum and are suitable for smaller sportfishing boats.

Baitboxes usually are portable ice chests where both rigged and unrigged baits are kept on ice to be used when ready. There should be stowage room for the baitboxes, as of course for rods and reels, while underway.

Equipment considered absolutely necessary on a big-game sportfishing boat includes a long-handled gaff, a wooden billy club—preferably weighted—and a tail rope. In addition, a flying gaff can prove invaluable on larger fish. The gaff is necessary for every species of big-game fish. Cloth gloves are necessary for grasping the wire leader and the rasplike bills of the marlin, sailfish and broadbill.

Communication equipment on the larger boats may include sophisticated marine radios, ship-to-shore radio telephones, radar gear and Loran for bad-weather and long-distance navigation. The bigger boats have room for elaborate depth-finding and fish-finding equipment. Many small sportfishing boats too today carry excellent small marine radios, including citizen's band sets, and compact depth-finders and fish-finders.

TACKLE

Rods, Reels and Lines

There is considerable leeway in this day and age for selection of big-game tackle. Fifty years ago, most big-game anglers had to rely on the huge, stout wooden rod, such as those built by Hardy, and heavy, big reels such as the Vom Hofe. But today, with excellent hollow tubular fiberglass rods and lightweight precision reels with reliable braking systems, an experienced angler can subdue a big fish with relatively light tackle.

Conventional saltwater rods differ from freshwater rods only in size and ability to handle large fish. Conventional tackle is generally considered to be the relatively short rod used with the level-winding reel. Decades ago, the most popular of the big-game rods were made of split bamboo, but fiberglass is now generally accepted as the best material for these rods. It makes an extremely strong and yet light rod which will not take a "set" and is almost impervious to salt water and corrosion. Roller guides are used almost exclusively now on the best big-game rods and perform the important function of reducing friction between the line and guide. Corrosion-proof guides and those made from stainless steel or Carboloy are preferable for big fish. Among the features to look for in a preferred big-game rod are a wooden butt section of excellent wood with a strongly made end ferrule to fit a fighting chair gimbal or a "Bimini belt" socket, and an equally corrosion-proof reelseat with strong locking rings to allow the rod tip to be locked into position and to keep the reel from working loose from the seat during action.

Spinning tackle, with monofilament lines in the 20–30-pound class, has been used with some success for big-game fish. Saltwater flyrods are used in many areas for some fish, such as tarpon. This kind of big-game fishing can be an exciting challenge for even the most experienced angler. However, many of the fish in the medium and heavier classes cannot be handled practically on either spinning or flyfishing gear, at least by the average angler. It is quite possible to take many big-game fish in the light class with spinning gear if one is experienced enough in the handling of the tackle, and a number of men have taken sailfish and white marlin on saltwater flyrods. But the majority of sportsmen use conventional gear.

The revolving-spool reel for saltwater big-game fishing has undergone some major changes in recent years. The two most widely used reels today fall into two categories. The older of the two has what is referred to as a "star drag" while the newer reels have a quadrant lever to achieve drag tension. Unlike the star drag, the quadrant lever is separate from and does not rotate with the spool-drive shaft. The star-drag reel is still widely used, but more of the newer reels are found on sportfishing craft today. The advantage of the lever-action drag is that the striking drag can be preset, giving the angler a distinct advantage. The exact drag needed for striking can be set or reset instantly under a number of varying conditions. Drag tension is of great importance in fighting large, fast-moving big-game fish — whether in setting the striking drag just before a strike, or resetting it after changing damaged baits or upon bringing a heavy fish to the boat.

Lines for big-game fishing are now manufactured in various classes in order to conform to International Game Fish Association regulations. These lines are classified by seven different breaking strengths: 6, 12, 20, 30, 50, 80, and 130 pounds.

The following chart gives the general recommended weights in ounces for big-game rods. It also shows the suggested reel size and line test for various species of big-game fish. Rod weights, measured at the rod tip, are given for modern glass rods.

Big-Game Fishing Tackle

LIGHT

Species	Reel size	Line test (lbs.)	Rod weight* (oz.)
Atlantic sailfish	2/0-4/0	12-20	6-9
Pacific sailfish	2/0-4/0	12-20	6-9
White marlin	2/0-4/0	12-20	6-9
Striped marlin	4/0	12-20	6-9
Blue marlin	6/0	20-50	9-16
Black marlin	6/0	30-50	12-16
Swordfish	6/0	30-50	12-16
Bluefin tuna (giant)	9/0	50	16-20

MEDIUM

Species	Reel size	Line test (lbs.)	Rod weight* (oz.)
Atlantic sailfish	4/0-6/0	20-30	9-12
Pacific sailfish	4/0-6/0	20-30	9-12
White marlin	4/0-6/0	20-30	9-12
Striped marlin	7/0	30-50	9-12
Blue marlin	9/0	50-80	16-24
Black marlin	9/0	50-80	16-24
Swordfish	9/0	50-80	16-24
Bluefin tuna (giant)	9/0	80	16-24

HEAVY

Species	Reel size	Line test (lbs.)	Rod weight* (oz.)
Atlantic sailfish	6/0	30-50	16-18
Pacific sailfish	6/0	30-50	16-18
White marlin	6/0	30-50	16-18
Striped marlin	9/0	80	18-20
Blue marlin	12/0	130	24-30
Black marlin	12/0	130	24-30
Swordfish	12/0	130	24-30
Bluefin tuna (giant)	12/0	130	24-30

*The rod weight as given is for the tip only in tubular glass construction. When using monofilaments, the heavier rod weights are suggested, because of the elasticity of the line.

Terminal Tackle

Terminal tackle—the tackle that exists between the snap swivel at the end of the line and the hook—is of the utmost importance in fighting large ocean fish. Considerable care should be taken in selecting good swivels, for a cheap, weak or defective swivel has caused the loss of many a fine fish. The ideal swivels are those operating on small bearings and made of stainless steel. They are slightly more expensive than the conventional brass or black swivel but hold up better and prevent line twist.

Double line—just above the leader—should be constructed and tied with a Bimini twist knot—allowing approximately 15 feet of double line for lines of 50-pound test and under and 30 feet of double line for the heavier line tests, such as 80- and 130-pound. It should be tied together every two or three feet with a few twists of dental floss, to keep it together so that it can easily pass through rod guides.

Wire leaders come in both braided cable and stainless steel. Both are about equal in strength for the length and weight. The braided-wire has less tendency to kink than stainless-steel, but it rusts more easily, especially in salt water.

Wire leader comes in either shiny or dull finish, and it is a matter of choice which one uses. The main thing to remember is that any kink in wire leader can weaken it to the point where it will easily break. As far as test strength is concerned, each roll of wire gives the breaking test on the package and it is wise to base the size wire leader you are going to use on the size and species of the fish sought. It is best to overestimate your fish's weight when deciding on the wire leader. Many a big fish has been lost because it hit a bait being trolled on leader meant for a smaller fish.

Nylon monofilament leader can be used too. It has no tendency to kink, but braided-wire and stainless-steel are almost impervious to cutting by sharp teeth, whereas nylon is much more vulnerable.

The simple table below can be followed to choose a leader strength. Nylon mono is made in so many grades and sizes that elaborate tables of diameters and breaking strains mean little, but the breaking strain is given on the package, as it is for cable and stainless leaders.

Tackle class	Species	IGFA line class (lbs.)	Mono leader (lbs.)	Wire leader (lbs.)
Very light	Atlantic sailfish	12-20	30-50	#3 (32)
Light	White marlin	30	80	#8 (86)
Medium	Blue marlin	50	120	#10 (128)
Heavy	Black marlin; swordfish	80	200	#12 (176)
Very heavy	Giant tuna	130	300	#15 (272)

Big-game hooks must take a tremendous strain, so it is wise to purchase good ones. The best hooks are made of high carbon steel-alloy wire and are plated with cadmium or tin to prevent rusting. The wire is hardened at 1550°F. and tempered at 750°F. The ring at the eye is formed by cold swaging, which reduces bulk at the eye. All large saltwater hooks today are forged. That is, after the hook has been made, the hook is hammered flat along both sides of the bend, while still hot, to give it additional strength. The appropriate hook size and pattern depends not only on the fish but the type of bait or rigging used. The following is a general guide:

Species	Hook size	Wire leader size	Mono leader size (lbs.)
Atlantic sailfish	7/0-8/0	#5-7	30
White marlin	7/0-9/0	#8-9	80
Pacific sailfish	8/0-9/0	#8-9	80
Striped marlin	8/0-9/0	#8-10	80
Blue marlin	9/0-10/0	#11-13	—
Swordfish	8/0-12/0	#11-13	—
Black marlin	9/0-12/0	#11-13	—
Bluefin tuna	10/0-12/0	#14-15	—

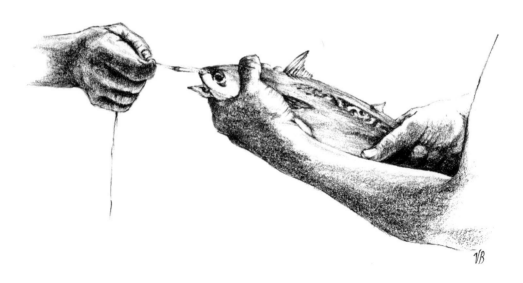

Bait

At the end of all your tackle, of course, must be something to interest the fish. One of the best all-round trolling baits is the mullet, which is found over much of the world. Although the mullet rarely enters the actual diet of big-game species (during an extensive study of sailfish stomach contents, for example, the only mullet remains found were "split" for baits), it has the durability required for ocean trolling. In areas where mullet are not abundant or do not occur at all, there are a number of good surface baits available. In Florida, the Bahamas, and elsewhere in the Caribbean the balao is an excellent bait for sailfish, white marlin and small blue marlin. It can be purchased in fresh and frozen form and is easily stored. However, it is not effective in taking the larger blue and black marlin; for these fish one uses bonito, bonefish, mackerel and even Allison tuna. Also, live or frozen squid can be used, as well as artificial squid lures. In addition, many artificial baits are manufactured today. There are as many commonly accepted methods of rigging baits for trolling as there are methods to use them. Strip baits are popular for some of the smaller billfish.

PLAYING AND BOATING THE FISH

The Strike

Perhaps the most crucial instant in all of big-game fishing is when the fish strikes the bait. Many times the fish will strike with such force—brought on by either hunger or anger—that it will hook itself. In that case, the angler does not have to decide how to strike; he is simply concerned with handling the fish properly now that it is hooked.

But many fish do not strike the trolled baits instantly; they prefer to take a close look at them before deciding to take one. It is this situation which can cause problems. Many times an angler will do well to free-spool the reel, allowing the bait to drop back behind the boat and to sink, perhaps causing the fish to think it hit the morsel and to decide to circle around and swallow it. On the other hand, when a fish can't seem to make up its mind to hit one of the baits, either speeding up the boat slightly or rapidly cranking the handle of the reel on the rod of the bait the fish is following may excite the fish, causing it to speed up and strike. Sometimes neither method works and the fish simply goes away without striking at all.

One thing is certain on the strike. It is wise for the angler to be watching the baits and preferably either seated in the chair or standing close to it when the strike comes. In this way the fisherman can grab whichever rod contains the line the fish hits and get ready to strike the fish himself—in order to set the hook—or a mate may hand him the proper rod and the butt can be quickly fitted into the chair gimbal. Many big-game fish are missed because the angler is too far away from the rod or chair when the strike comes. Big-game fish do not strike as often as smaller species of fish, and an angler may go many hours or even days and not get a strike. But when a big-game fish does strike, there is very little time in which to make the correct moves. It is best to be ready.

Many skippers and mates have their own opinion

about the preferred striking drag for different reels, lines and species of fish, but a rough chart can be made up that will serve generally for most cases. A general rule could be that the striking drag should be set to not less than 20 percent or more than 40 percent of the line's maximum test strength. A simple pocket-sized fish-weighing scale can be used to measure the pound test of the line at the tip, after the rod has been set in a gunwale rod holder. The chart would look approximately like this:

Rod class	Line test (lbs.)	Reel	Capacity (yards)	Species	Striking drag (lbs.)
Very light	12	2/0	475	Atlantic sailfish	4
	20	3/0	500	Atlantic sailfish	5
Light	30	4/0	500	White marlin	7
Medium	50	6/0	575	Blue marlin	20
Heavy	80	9/0	600	Black marlin Swordfish	25-30
Very heavy	130	12/0	750	Giant tuna	40

If the skipper, the mate and the angler are certain the fish has taken the bait, there are several options open. If the angler is inexperienced, it is best to take the advice of the skipper or mate. In many cases, knowing their own waters and the habits of the fish there, they will slow the boat down almost to idle, and will allow the fish to take the bait and circle down to a depth where it is allowed to turn the bait around and swallow it. It is an unnerving experience for a novice to have a crew tell him to wait for a ten- or fifteen-second count before striking, but occasionally this is best. Big-game fishing crews in many parts of the world, and particularly off the west coast of Mexico, use this system. At the end of the count, the skipper will gun the engines of the boat to take up slack. The angler then lowers his rod tip almost horizontally and strikes once or twice, hard, by bringing the rod up sharply to vertical.

In other areas of the world, crews may use a different system. For example, some Bahamian skippers seem to prefer to speed up the boat as soon as the slashing bill of the fish has struck the bait and the line has fallen to the surface of the water from the outrigger clips. Many of them feel this will succeed in hooking the fish at the instant it swallows the bait. In contrast, many sportsmen, feeling that an angler should fight his fish on more equal terms, prefer to see the skipper put the engine in neutral as soon as the fish is hooked. This is somewhat moot, but this method is required in the Palm Beach Masters Tournament, for example.

At any rate, most conventional techniques of fighting big-game fish today involve the use of the boat as much as the rod and reel. It has been said by many of the pros that more big-game fish are caught by the man at the wheel of a sportfisherman than by the angler in the chair. There is no arguing that a good combination of skipper, mate and angler is hard to beat when it comes to landing big-game fish.

Tiring the Fish

Big-game fish—almost without exception—will make their most frantic and longest run right after being hooked. Depending upon the size and condition of the fish, it may take out anywhere from several hundred to more than a thousand yards of line in a matter of minutes. With marlin or sailfish one can expect a heart-stopping series of acrobatic jumps as the fish clears the surface repeatedly in an effort to get rid of the hook. In the case of the bluefin and yellowfin tuna, there will be no jumping, but tremendous bursts of strength as the fish streaks away and downward. In both these cases, the angler is advised to keep the rod tip up to let the bending rod absorb the shock. This is the moment, as the pressure on the line increases progressively as more of it leaves the spool rapidly, where most fish are lost. They are lost because the lines break from too much strain alone or because the angler becomes too worried about his fast-disappearing line and increases the drag, hoping to slow it down. It is better to have a lot of line out. The drag of the line being pulled through the water will do more than anything else at this time to slow down the fish.

When the fish has stopped its initial run and begins to swim, then the angler can begin to regain the lost line. The fish may jump any number of times after that, but the slight decrease in drag as it makes its runs will lessen the chances of losing a fish. Regaining line on a fish is a matter of pumping properly. The rod is raised or pumped when the slack is taken up. It is quickly lowered while the reel handle is pumped to gain slack, then pumped or raised again. The reel handle should not be turned while the rod is being raised to regain line. It will simply cause the drag to slip unnecessarily, losing rather than gaining line.

The mate will have reeled in the other lines to give the angler room to fight the fish without becoming entangled. The advantage of the swiveling chair becomes apparent to a novice big-game fisherman when he feels the mate constantly turning the chair so that he is at all times facing the direction where the line slants out to the fish. This permits the angler to balance his weight.

It is during this stage that the captain of the boat can help or hinder a fisherman by the way he handles the boat. If the angler is tiring and the fish is either swimming down and away from the boat or sounding, the skipper may "back down" on the fish by putting the boat into reverse, thus taking considerable strain off the back and arms of the angler and allowing him time to gain line on the fish. Other skippers, following a different battle plan, may turn the boat and run parallel to the swimming fish, allowing the angler to reduce the drag slightly and causing a billow to form in the line between the boat and the fish. This exerts tremendous pressure on the fish, causing it to tire far more rapidly than the backing-down method, which is really more to spare the angler than to tire the fish.

It is at this stage, particularly if an angler is a novice at the game and is feeling the strain in the back and arms, that a harness can ease the pressure. Slipped under the angler, it fits snugly around the lower back, in the kidney region. It has canvas or leather straps which can be snapped to rings on both sides of the reel. This allows the angler to absorb the powerful pull of the big fish with the back and leg muscles.

When playing a big-game fish on spinning tackle there is great danger of breaking the line, and considerable care should be taken to watch the drag setting on the reel. The most common mistake is to tighten up the drag as the fish takes out more line. The angler's reaction should be just the opposite. The tension on the line increases by itself as the diameter of the line left on the spool decreases, and so the drag should be loosened rather than tightened. Also, line being pulled through the water creates tremendous resistance, which is hard on the fish but hard on the line as well. So the standard procedure on most billfish is to loosen the drag and raise the rod tip high when the fish is making a run. This will relieve the line of some strain, but the bend of the rod and the drag of the line through the water will continue to tire the fish.

Bringing It In

As the fish gets closer and closer to the boat, the angler can roughly judge its depth by the angle of line slanting from the rod tip to the fish. As the angle from the vertical lessens quickly, one can expect the fish to surface and jump. It is then that the rod tip should be held high to absorb the strain of the thrashing jump and also to prevent slack from forming, which might allow the fish to throw the hook.

Usually, big-game fish will sound toward the end of a battle, going as deep as 1,000 feet or more. They may even die down there from the exertion of the battle, from pressure, or from the combination. There are two options for the angler, depending upon his own physical condition, the size of the fish and the length of the fight.

One is to have the boat move directly over the fish and try to pump it up. This can require hours of difficult work, particularly if the fish is large or dead. Many skippers think this attracts sharks, particularly if the fish is bleeding. The other option is to move the boat several hundred yards ahead of the fish, preferably with the drag reduced to avoid putting any additional stress on the line. Then the angler resets his drag and begins to lift the fish up again. At an angle rather than straight down, the line tilts the head of the fish up as it is pulled, planing it up rather than pulling it. Many sportfishing skippers utilize this method.

If the fish is not dead, or if it does not sound for long, and is now obviously tired and coming in to the boat, several things can happen which will greatly affect the angler's chance of boating it. Most billfish are extremely strong fighters and will make last-minute jumps quite close to the boat when the novice angler least expects it. This is the time when most billfish are lost; the angler allows slack to form in the line and the fish throws the hook. At this point the rod tip should be held as high as possible. A fish jumping close to the boat is also more likely to get itself tail-wrapped by the wire leader.

The snap swivel fastened to the wire leader will finally appear. This is the signal for the boating process to begin, because the snap swivel cannot pass through the roller guides at the rod tip. That is as close to the boat as the angler can bring the fish with the rod. It is then up to the mate to reach out, preferably with gloved hands, take the leader, and lead the tired fish close to the side of the boat near the stern. There he will grasp the bill or use his gaff. If the fish is very large or if it is wanted for mounting, the skipper or another member of the crew will either whack it across the forehead with a weighted wooden billy club or stun it temporarily while a tail rope is pulled tight at the slender area at the base of the tail. The skipper or other crew member may also have gaffed the fish to prevent it wrenching itself free from the man holding the bill. If the fish is to be tagged for migration studies or is not wanted for mounting, it will be released. In that case it is not gaffed or struck with the club, nor is a tail rope fastened to it. The numbered tag is inserted in the musculature at the base of the dorsal fin and the wire leader is snipped off close to the eye of the hook. A combination of salt water and stomach acids will erode the hook in time, and some other big-game angler will have a chance to battle the fish another day.

If the fish is to be boated, it is either taken aboard through the transom door, pulled over the gunwales if it is small enough, or hoisted tail-first by a rope fastened to the snap of the gin pole.

The moments of boating a big-game fish can be very dangerous for anglers and crew members who are not experienced. A slash of the bill or a swipe of the large sickle-shaped tail can cause serious injury. It is better for the angler to stay in the chair—even if he is experienced—while the crew is going about the business of boating the fish. Crew members and anglers in the cockpit should be extremely careful not to step into any coils of line or leader while the fish is being held alongside. If a big fish breaks loose from the man holding the bill or the gaff and someone is fouled in the line, he may be pulled overboard. The angler should set his drag on the very light position during this time. If the fish does get loose and make a last-ditch run, it will have less chance of snapping the line than if the drag is on full position.

KITE FISHING

The use of kites dates back to natives of Polynesia centuries ago. Many years ago anglers on the West Coast, in the area of Catalina Island, tried the system, and following that the great fishing guide Tommy Gifford utilized it off Florida and the Bahamas.

It was not until Bob Lewis, of Kendall, Florida, produced them commercially that fishing kites really caught the fancy of the average fisherman. They still are not widely known in the northern part of the United States or portions of the West Coast or Great Lakes. The largest collection of kite-fishing devotees is still in the Florida area—where the weather is ideal most of the year for this type of fishing.

The use of kites is a complete departure from the traditional, and very successful, method of taking big-game fish by trolling. It incorporates the use of fishing with live bait with the use of an outrigger—the outrigger in this case being the kite line itself. The boat is not kept in motion as it is while trolling; however, it is kept idling in many cases so that it can get underway in case a big fish hits the baits.

The theory of kite fishing is to use a system of surface angling for big-game fish where there is no line in the water or on the surface between the boat and the bait. Also, devotees of the sport feel that live baits—allowed to swim naturally on or just below the surface—attract the game fish better than dead trolled baits. Live-bait fishing has been done for as long as man has fished, but it has always been difficult to keep a bait on the surface where the strike can be seen by the angler in time to strike back at the attacking fish. Live bait fished deep also takes game fish, but the angler does not know the fish has struck until he feels the strike as a tightening of the line, sometimes too late to set the hook.

Also billfish are surface or close-to-the-surface feeders, as are many species of game fish. Kite fishermen have noticed that bait fish hooked through the meaty part of the body—so as not to injure the backbone—send out distress signals when swimming on or just below the surface. These signals are picked up for a considerable distance by predators and result in slashing strikes which are truly spectacular. Kingfish, wahoo, barracuda and dolphin take swimming surface kite baits at full speed, sometimes shooting high into the air as they take the live fish. Billfish and tuna hit these baits without the careful scrutiny they sometimes give the trolled baits, hooking themselves solidly. The slack line from the rod tip to the clip on the kite line and down to the swimming live bait apparently allows just enough room for the fish to hook itself before the line is taken up by the reel. Finally, the boat can be allowed to drift with the engine or motor off, so there is no sound or vibration to alert game fish to the presence of a fishing boat.

There is the problem of keeping bait alive, which is not necessary in the trolled-bait system; this may be the reason many charterboat skippers do not specialize in kite fishing. But those professionals who do, and those private fishermen who have been sold on the sport, have managed to solve the problem of keeping the bait alive with not too much trouble. There are a number of inexpensive oxygen-supplying pumps which work off regular boat batteries or even flashlight batteries and can supply a bucket or box of live bait with enough air to live for days. A live-bait box that will circulate seawater to fish can be built at the stern of the boat.

The choice of small bait fish is up to the individual, but those who have practiced the sport for years tend to lean toward the pilchard, the pinfish, and the blue runner in Florida, the Bahamas, and elsewhere in the Caribbean—although many other small fish will serve as well. In northern waters the porgy is a favorite. Live eels can be used in the surf when the kites are used to fish off a beach rather than from a boat. An offshore wind, however, is necessary for this system to work.

The same basic tackle is used in kite fishing as is used in conventional trolling. If big-game fish are being sought—and any species of big-game fish may be taken with kites—the same rod weights, reel sizes and line test should be used. Saltwater spinning tackle can be adapted well to kite fishing. The rod may be held in the hand or rested in a rod holder, but drag should be set fairly light to prevent the rod from being jerked from the rod holder in case of a sudden and unexpected strike by a large fish. The angler or a crew member should man the large reel holding the kite line at all times. This is because the baits should be kept swimming on or just below the surface, and any sudden gust of wind can elevate the kite and raise the bait fish high above the water, where it will wriggle in the air and attract nothing. A few turns of the kite spool will lower it back into the water. The opposite is true when the wind dies down and the bait swims too deep. A few turns of the spool will bring it back up to the surface.

When the wind dies down to calm or almost to calm, there is not much one can do about flying a kite by itself. One method of using kites in no-wind conditions is to troll with them as outriggers. The kite may be flown on the downwind side of the boat out to as much distance as the kite line will allow. Dead trolled baits may be skipped across the surface, much the same way as with the conventional outrigger, but they can be run much farther from the boat wake. Many kite fishermen troll rigged mullet and balao baits approximately 100 feet off the side of a trolling boat.

Another system of keeping kites aloft on calm days has been refined by such skippers as Captain Allen Self of North Key Largo, Florida. He uses helium balloons fastened to the kites on no-wind days or days with not enough wind to keep a regular kite aloft.

Commercially made kites come in light, medium, and heavy models, for varying winds. Homemade kites can be built the same way. Here is how the basic kite is constructed.

The construction of the kite reel spool is simple for any handy angler. The crude reel—about a foot in diameter—can be constructed from two circular plates of plywood glued or nailed to a smaller wooden plate inside. It can be turned by crank and should be able to carry a minimum of 150 feet of heavy thread line. (Thread is best, although mono can be used.) The reel is mounted on a broomstick handle, one part protruding below to fit into a rod holder and the other sticking up above the reel with a screw eye or rod guide at the end to let the line run out.

Made of light silk or nylon, the kite dries relatively fast in wind after rain or a dunking. The crosspieces are made of either new or used sections of fiberglass fishing rods. The cloth is fastened to the hollow ends of the rod blanks by sewing a regular dress hook at each corner of the silk so that it hooks into the end of the blank. The kite should be about 3 by 3 feet. The kite line should be fastened to it by a harness from all four corners and by a line connected to the crosspieces in the very center (tied to a fishing swivel to keep it stable). The kite line should be fairly heavy, at least 50-pound.

Two regular swivels, one smaller than the other, should be inserted in the kite line—one 50 feet from the kite and one at 100 feet. There should be at least another 50 feet of kite line between the last swivel and the spool to allow the last swivel to move out to about 50 feet from the boat.

Two regular wooden spring clothespins should slide along the kite line. The clothespin nearest the kite should have a small hole bored through it so neither swivel will pass through it. This means that the first swivel to hit it—the one 50 feet from the kite—will carry the clothespin with it. Then an ordinary U-shaped brad or half paper clip should be clamped in the jaws of the clothespin and the line from the first fishing rod passed through the staple so that it moves freely back and forth. If a fish strikes, the brad will pull from the jaws of the clothespin and the line will fall free to the surface.

The second clothespin should have a larger hole drilled through it, so that the first swivel is allowed to pass through, but not the larger second swivel. Thus, the second swivel will stop this clothespin 100 feet from the tip of the line. The second brad and the next fishing line is fastened to this one. Then the reel is allowed to let out about 50 feet more of kite line until two lines dangle from it, running freely through the clothespin-held brads 50 and 100 feet from the boat.

There are times when the kite will get dunked by a sudden drop in breeze—before the boat can be speeded up enough to keep it aloft. Having several kites along is a good idea.

The rod holder or seat for the kite should be strong, because the strain on the kite reel shaft is considerable.

The wind pushing the kite exerts more pressure than is commonly realized, particularly when used in trolling.

It is not necessary for the angler or another crew member to reel in the second fishing line when a fish strikes the first bait. Since there is no line in the water, there is almost no way the line can be fouled.

Appendix B
The IGFA Rules

If you are in a tournament or if you think you may have a record fish on, there are several things to remember. No one on the boat can assist the angler during the fight by touching him in any way or helping with the rod or reel. The mate may turn the chair for the angler, and other people aboard can hand him objects if he asks for them, such as a cold drink, a seat harness, or a rod belt. When the fish is brought to the boat, the mate may take the leader wire, but until then the angler is on his own.

Upon reaching the dock or marina, the fish should be weighed officially and the proper forms should be filled out. The fish should be measured to ensure proper mounting. The test of the line and the type of bait should be recorded. And aside from their use as evidence, it is not a bad idea to have a few photographs taken. Such moments may not happen often in an angler's lifetime.

The IGFA rules follow. Mr. Elwood K. Harry, Executive Vice President of the International Game Fish Association, has kindly given me permission to reprint them.

RULES GOVERNING RECORD CATCHES

All IGFA angling rules are voted on by the Officers, Executive Committee, International Committee, and angling Clubs with current IGFA membership status. Records are only kept on Marine species.

All claims for an IGFA World Record catch must be approved by at least two Officers or members of the Executive Committee before being acknowledged as a World Record.

Questionable or protested applications for World Records will be referred to the full Executive Committee. Such catches will be removed from the Chart until a decision is reached.

No claim will be considered unless it is accompanied by the correct amount and kind of line sample.

In case of a disputed identification two competent ichthyologists will be called upon to make the decision. If there is a question, the angler will be notified and given ample opportunity to send in further identification.

In some instances, an Officer or member of an IGFA committee or a deputy from a local Member Club may be asked to re-check information supplied on a claim. Such action is not to be regarded as doubt of the formal affidavit, but is merely an evidence of the extreme care and accuracy with which the IGFA tries to maintain its World Record Charts.

To replace a record for a fish weighing 100 pounds or more, the replacement must weigh at least one pound (16 ounces) more than the existing record. A catch exceeding the existing record by less than one pound will be considered a tie with the existing record. In case of a tie claim involving more than two catches, weight must be compared with the *Lowest* weight involved in the existing records, but nothing *less* is a claim.

To replace a record for a fish weighing less than 100 pounds, the replacement must weigh at least one-half pound (8 ounces) more than the existing record. A catch exceeding the existing record by less than half a pound will be considered a tie with the existing record.

No estimated weights will be accepted.

Time Limit on Claims

Claims for fish caught in Continental U.S. waters will not be accepted by the International Game Fish Association if the date of the catch is more than *60 days* before the date of receipt of the claim by the IGFA. Claims for fish caught in other waters will not be accepted if the date of the catch is more than *three months* before the date of receipt of the claim by the IGFA.

If a claim for a record is entered without full particulars, a period of two months is allowed during which the IGFA shall make an effort to complete the claim, and after which time, if the claim still remains incomplete, the catch shall be discarded as a claimant for a record.

When a new species of fish is made eligible for a record, the date of the announcement will be the effective date, and time limit on claims will be as of that date. No prior catches will be considered. Appearance of the name of such a fish upon the Record Chart for the first time will be considered proper notification in lieu of any other notice.

Scales

All record fish should be weighed on scales that have been checked and certified for accuracy by Government agencies or other qualified and accredited organizations. All scales should be checked and certified at least once each six months.

If at the time of weighing the fish, the scale has not been properly certified within six months, it should be checked for accuracy as quickly as possible, and a report included with the application *stating the findings* of the inspector prior to any adjustments of the scale.

If a properly certified scale is not available, the scale must be checked by weighing objects of recognized and proven poundage. This type of weight check must be at least equal to the weight of the fish. Any type scale may be used as long as its accuracy can be established.

No fish weighed only at sea will be accepted as a claim for an IGFA record.

A fish must be weighed by an official weighmaster, if one is available, or by a recognized local or IGFA official. Disinterested witnesses to the weight should be used whenever possible.

At the time of weighing the actual tackle used must be exhibited to the weighmaster and weight witness.

No estimated weights will be accepted.

Preparation of Record Claims

Record applications will only be accepted for the class of line actually used in catching the fish. If the line overtests, the application will be considered in the next higher class. If the line undertests into a lower class, the application will not be considered for the lower line class. The highest pound test line permissible is 130-pound class. If the line test on an All Tackle claim overtests 130 pounds, it will be considered as an All Tackle record only and will be listed as such if approved.

The angler must fill in all items on the application personally, and the Association urges that the angler send in his own affidavit, line sample and photographs. The line sample should be submitted in a manner that it can be unwound without damage to the line. A recommended method is to take a rectangular piece of stiff cardboard and cut a notch in opposite ends. Secure one end to the cardboard and wind the line on the cardboard in the notched areas. Secure the other end and identify it. Also, place your name on the cardboard. Do not submit the line in a hank.

Extreme care should be exercised in measuring the fish, as the measurements are usually important for other scientific studies.

The angler is responsible for seeing that the necessary *signatures* of boat captain, weighmaster and witnesses are on the claim. If an IGFA officer, or member of the IGFA Executive or International Committee, or officer of a Member Club is available, he or she should be asked to witness the claim. The name of a boatman, guide, or weighmaster repeated as witness will not be acceptable.

The application form must be used in filing claims and must be accompanied by the mandatory yardage (see Angling Rules) of actual line used. The application form may be reproduced. The application form and line sample originally submitted will be the only one considered. It is of the utmost importance that application forms be filled in carefully and correctly.

The angler must appear in person to have his application notarized. In territories where notarization is not possible or customary, the signature of a government Commissioner or Resident, a member of Embassy, Legation or Consular staff, or an Officer or member of the Executive or International committees of the IGFA may replace notarization.

Any deliberate falsification of an application will disqualify the applicant for any future record!

Photographs

Photographs of the fish, the rod and reel used to make the catch and the scale used to weigh the fish shall accompany each record application. A photograph of the angler with the fish is also desired. Shark photographs should also include a photo of the head and the nature of the front teeth. Enough pictures must be submitted to identify the species without a doubt. This is especially important with the marlin, bass, shark, and tuna species.

Photographs should be taken of the fish in a hanging position and also lying on a flat surface on its side. In both types of photograph, no part of the fish should be obscured. When hanging, the fish should be broadside to the camera with all fins, tip of the jaws, sword or spear clearly shown. Do not hold the tip of any fin. Do not stand in front of the fish; also do not hold the fish.

When photographing a fish lying on its side, the surface beneath the fish should be smooth and a ruler or marked tape placed beside the fish if possible. Photographs from various angles are most helpful. An *additional* photograph of the fish on the scale and showing the weight helps in expediting the application.

ANGLING RULES

1. Any fish caught by any method of fishing in accordance with IGFA rules is eligible for a record

claim if it outweighs the existing record by the required amount in its line class. The rod, reel and all other tackle must be in reasonable proportion, or "balance" to the line size.

2. The IGFA record classes are: All-Tackle (an All-Tackle record is the heaviest fish caught on any of the line classes listed); 12-pound line class (line testing up to and including 12 pounds); 20-pound line class (line testing more than 12 pounds and up to and including 20 pounds); 30-pound line class; 50-pound line class; 80-pound line class; 130-pound line class.

3. Record classes are based on the wet testing strength of the actual line used in making the catch. All line testing is conducted in a nationally recognized laboratory in accordance with Spec. CCC-T-191b, Method 4102. All claims for records in line classes less than 50 pounds must be accompanied by 50 feet (including the entire double) of the actual line used in making the catch. For line classes of 50 pounds or more, 80 feet (including the entire double) must be submitted. The line sample must be in one piece. Backing: If two lines of different test strength, *spliced or tied together* are used in taking a fish, that catch shall be classified under the heavier of the two lines and a sample of both lines must be submitted. NOTE: The IGFA tests lines only in connection with applications for records.

4. The leader and the double line on all weights of tackle up to and including the 50-pound line class, shall be limited to 15 feet of double line and 15 feet of leader. For heavier tackle, the line shall not be doubled at the leader end for more than 30 feet, and the leader shall not exceed 30 feet. There are no minimum lengths. Also, the use of a double line or leader is not required. The length of the leader shall be the overall length including any legal hook arrangement attached thereto. A double line must be the doubling of the actual line used. The leader may not be lengthened to compensate for a shorter double, and the

double line may not be lengthened commensurately for a shorter leader. The double line and the leader must be connected with a knot, snap or a swivel. There are no limits to the material or strength of the leader. When the leader is brought to within the grasp of the mate, or the end of the leader is wound to the rod tip, more than one person is permitted to hold the leader, and there is no restriction regarding the use of a gaffer in addition to the persons holding the leader.

5. Rods must be in accordance with sporting ethics and customs. Considerable latitude is allowed, but rods giving the angler an unsporting advantage will be disqualified. The rule is intended to eliminate the use of freak rods, and to act as a means of protection to anglers. The minimum length of the rod tip is 50 inches, and the maximum length of the rod butt is 27 inches. These measurements shall be made from a point directly beneath the center of the reel. A curved butt is measured in a straight line. These limitations do not apply to surf casting rods used in surf casting.

6. Reels must be in accordance with sporting ethics and customs. Mechanical reels of any nature are prohibited. This would include ratchet handle reels, motor, hydraulic or electrically driven reels or any other device giving the angler an unfair advantage. The use of double handled reels is prohibited.

7. Fighting chairs may have no mechanical device which aids the angler in fighting a fish. Gimbals must be free-swinging which also allows a gimbal swinging only in a vertical plane. Any gimbal which allows the angler to reduce strain or to rest while fighting is prohibited.

8. Metal lines, including metal core lines, are prohibited.

9. For bait fishing no more than two single hooks may be separately attached to the leader or trace, and then only if both hooks are firmly imbedded or attached to the bait. The eyes of the hooks must be at

least an overall hook's length apart and no more than 18 inches. A hook's length is the full overall length of the largest of the two hooks. The use of a dangling or swinging hook is prohibited. A so-called "Bottom Rig" for fishing on or close to the bottom is acceptable if it consists of no more than two single hooks on separate leaders with both hooks imbedded in the respective baits and separated sufficiently so that a fish caught on one hook cannot be foul hooked by the other. All claims on two hook tackle must be accompanied by a photograph or sketch of the hook arrangement.

9a. In using a "teaser type" artificial lure with a skirt or trailing material, no more than two single hooks may be separately attached to the leader or trace. The eyes of the hooks must be an overall hook's length apart and no further than 12 inches apart. A hook's length is the full overall length of the largest of the two hooks. The trailing hook may not extend more than a hook's length beyond the skirt of the lure. A photograph showing the hook arrangement must accompany every application.

10. The use of a plug or other artificial lure with gang hooks is permitted. This use shall be limited to a total of two hooks either single, double, treble or any combination thereof. Hooks must be permanently and directly attached to the lure. All double and treble hooks must be free-swinging. The use of any plug or artificial lure with gang hooks is limited to casting and retrieving in a conventional manner. When casting from a boat, the boat must not be under any form of mechanical propulsion. With record applications, a photograph of the plug or lure must be submitted, and if it is not completely satisfactory the plug itself may be requested.

11. The use of any float is prohibited other than a small balloon or cork, which may be attached to the line or leader for the sole purpose of regulating the depth of the bait or for drifting of the bait.

12. Entangling devices, either with or without a hook, are prohibited.

13. A gaff not exceeding 8 feet in overall length may be used for boating a fish. In the case of a flying or detachable gaff, the rope may not exceed 30 feet. Only a single, fixed hook is permitted. The gaff rope shall be measured from the point where it is secured to the detachable head to the other end. Only the effective length shall be considered. If a fixed head gaff is used, the same limitations shall apply, and the gaff rope shall be measured from the same location on the gaff hook. No harpoon type attachments are permissible. The gaff length limitation does not apply when fishing from a bridge or pier.

14. The angler must hook, fight, and bring the fish to gaff unaided by any other person. If a rod holder is used and a fish strikes that bait, the angler must remove the rod from the rod holder as quickly as possible. (Note C, Rule 18 below.) The intent of this rule is that the angler, rather than anyone else, should hook and strike the fish.

15. Resting the rod on the gunwale of a boat while playing a fish is prohibited. Harness may be attached to reel or rod. The use of a rod belt is permitted. Replacing or adjusting the harness by another person is permitted.

16. Changing of rod or reel, splicing the line, or removal or addition thereto during the playing of a fish is prohibited.

17. In the event of a multiple strike fought by a single angler, only the first fish fought will be considered for a record.

18. The following acts or omissions will disqualify a catch:
   A. Failure to comply with the rules or tackle specifications.
   B. A broken rod that alters the effective length of the butt or tip beyond limitations or severely impairs the angling characteristics of the rod.
   C. Acts of persons other than the angler in ad-

justing reel drag or touching any part of the tackle either by hand or other device during the playing of the fish, or giving aid other than taking the leader (or trace) for gaffing purposes.

D. Handlining or using a handline or rope attached in any manner to a line or leader for the purpose of holding or lifting a fish.

E. Shooting, harpooning or lancing any fish, including sharks, at any stage of the catch.

F. Mutilations caused by sharks, other fish or propellers that remove or penetrate the flesh. (Injuries caused by leader or line, scratches, old healed scars and regeneration deformities shall not be considered disqualifying injuries.) Any mutilations on the fish must be explained completely in a separate report accompanying the application.

G. Chumming with flesh, blood, skin or guts of mammals is prohibited; however, any chumming with whole or parts of fish is permitted provided the chum is allowed to float without restraint. Live chum may be restrained.

H. Beaching or driving into shallow water any fish hooked from a boat, in order to deprive said fish of its normal ability to swim, is prohibited.

19. Only fish caught in accordance with the above rules shall be accepted as record claims by the International Game Fish Association.